MOTHER ANONYMOUS

MOTHER ANONYMOUS
BABIES.BOTTLES.BREAKDOWNS

Amanda Tilper

Tilper House Press
Ferndale, MI

Published by Tilper House Press
Ferndale, Michigan

ISBN: 979-8-9953768-0-4 (paperback)
ISBN: 979-8-9953768-2-8 (ebook)

First Edition
Printed in the United States of America

For all of the mothers out there that feel alone – I'm right here holding your hand.

"We are all broken. That's how the light gets in."
—Ernest Hemingway

INTRODUCTION

Before everything fell apart, I clung to a moment in the nursery at 3 a.m., where the air was filled with the scent of diaper cream and Dreft, and the Hatch light offered a dim glow. I rocked my wailing baby, with hot tears streaming down my cheeks. In that vulnerable space, I whispered, *'I can't do this. I don't want to be a mom anymore.'* The words felt real, and the guilt was immediate, but what lingered was the sense of despair, hanging above me like a crib mobile. It was my first indication that motherhood would diverge drastically from my expectations. The negative self-talk insidiously intensified: I didn't deserve the role of motherhood or this beautiful baby, it insisted relentlessly, whispering that I would never be good enough. Misery seemed inescapable as I repeatedly told myself there was no way out. I found myself angrily asking God, 'Why are you punishing me? What did I do to deserve this?' My past mistakes haunted me, and hope felt like an intangible concept. Yet, amid this darkness, there was a flicker of something else—a fragile whisper promising that healing was possible. That promise clung to me, quietly asserting that each small step taken was part of a journey toward restoration, providing a silver thread of hope woven through the raw reality of postpartum struggles.

Nobody warns you how rapidly your sense of self can vanish once your baby is born. It's shocking: your pre-childbirth identity disappears, replaced by someone you don't know—even to yourself. You are no longer you, while everyone else seems oblivious to the change. Gradually, self-care slips away unnoticed, and invisibility creeps in. I felt like a background character in my own life. Everyone focused on the baby—her sleep, diapers, milestones. My slipping identity was evident daily: stale milk on my clothes, greasy hair in every reflection. I carefully curated Instagram stories, trying to hide the dark circles and sorrow. When people asked, 'How are you?' I'd say, 'Tired, but blessed.' Inside, I wanted to reply, 'I'm pretty sure I'm in hell, and I can't escape.' I felt isolated and wished someone would reassure me these intense emotions were common, not a sign I was losing my mind, and that they wouldn't last forever. The accumulation of all this led to a pervasive loneliness and a deeper internal struggle.

The chaos of the pandemic intensified the stress of

motherhood, and doubts crept in more often. *Was I a bad mother? Why was my baby always crying? Why wasn't anyone rescuing me?* Each day, resentment toward my husband grew. It felt as if he'd left me stranded in a warzone, ill-equipped to survive. The negative buzzing in my head grew louder, drowning out anything good. Over time, hopelessness settled in. I became angry at God and blamed him for making life feel impossible.

One day—who knows which, since time blurs together when you're a new mother—I poured a glass of wine: just one. It was a cool, crisp Sauvignon Blanc, not too dry, not too sweet. I told myself I had earned it. That's what we hear, right? You survive the day, and there's your gold star in a wine glass. Without some kind of reward, all the hard work seems to go unnoticed. As someone who was dying for acknowledgement, I needed to be noticed. That drink became both a marker of survival and, as I'd soon learn, a new habit solidifying itself.

That glass at the end of the day became a ritual. At first, it soothed me, creating a sense of reward after a long day. Over time, the emotional effects shifted: what started as a treat evolved into a necessity. I realized that instead of truly coping with my days, I was just enduring until I could have my next drink. Anxiety began slicing through me during the day, manifesting as a tightness in my chest and an uncontrolled shaking in my hands. The only relief I seemed to recognize was found in that glass I reached for. However, the very thing that used to comfort me started to become the thing breaking me. The ritual of drinking, once uplifting, had become a driver of anxiety and a signal of lost control. Dependence crept in quietly, shifting my emotional state from comfort and relief to anxiety and entrapment.

But amidst this overwhelming sense of being trapped, there were moments, however small, where I tried to challenge the cycle. One evening, I decided to skip the usual drink, took a deep breath, and stepped outside to watch the sunset. The air felt different, cleaner, and it was a decision not driven by fear but by a flicker of hope. It didn't erase the anxiety, but it reminded me that I still had a choice, however fleeting it seemed. Such small acts granted me glimpses of agency, signaling that change was still within reach, even if I didn't yet fully believe it. These moments began to shape a new normal.

That became my new reality.

When the dust of postpartum began to settle—or maybe

just swirl in a different direction—I noticed a new kind of emptiness after giving up wine. I realized I was missing not just alcohol, but also the emotional relief it signaled: the day had ended, I'd survived, and I could finally rest. I genuinely enjoyed the taste of a crisp Sauvignon Blanc and the fizz of champagne. When the bottle was empty, my feelings were mixed: restlessness, fatigue, and a sense of contradiction. I felt torn between longing for comfort and recognizing my growing discomfort with dependency, which left me unsure of how to move forward emotionally.

Peter and I met on a cool night in May of 2019. I remember everything about our first date, as it was one of the best I had ever had. We laughed endlessly and said goodbye with an urgency to see each other again. Eight months after our first date—over drinks, of course—I was pregnant. I remember the exact day I took a pregnancy test: it was National Margarita Day. We had gone to my favorite Mexican restaurant to celebrate the holiday. When we returned to Peter's house, I took a test, sure I wasn't pregnant. I stood near the sink. He sat at the table, both of us silent—too stunned to speak. Overwhelmed with the idea of becoming parents after less than a year together, with our relationship carrying a certain toxicity from early on. Two months later, we were all hiding at home and wearing masks. In less than a year, I went from being employed full-time to planning a family with my on-again, off-again boyfriend, moving in with him during a global pandemic. Big life changes. The thought of a margarita after finding out I had a baby inside me was enough to keep me sober. I say sober lightly because I still didn't believe I had a problem.

The world shut down, but we were expected to keep going—especially as moms-to-be. I'd pictured my husband by my side at prenatal appointments, friends over to celebrate, and family visits to share the joy. Instead, COVID-19 restrictions made pregnancy lonely and sometimes scary. Like so many others, I went to every appointment alone, sharing updates with loved ones over FaceTime. It was nothing as I'd imagined.

Those months felt like limbo—physically present but emotionally checked out. Milestones I'd dreamed of celebrating with loved ones turned into silence or blurry video calls. Drive-by showers replaced gatherings, and hugs were delivered through screens. I grieved the experience I thought I'd have, layered on top of the constant anxiety about what was happening in the world.

We lived near downtown. All around, restaurants, bars, breweries, and a distillery beckoned within walking distance. A sprawling patio drew crowds—people wandered with drinks in hand, lingering among sidewalk sales. Day drinking set the tone. Alcohol surrounded me: easy access, liquor stores at every corner. It was constant, whether I registered it or not. Before pregnancy, my husband and I attended happy hours, wine and cocktail events, and sipped craft drinks. After kids, I didn't feel angry about missing out—just a twinge of sadness. Others seemed to have more fun. Eventually, I found ways to involve my children in these rituals, pulling them into my addiction.

After both of my girls were born in 2020 and 2022, I found reasons (or excuses) to justify drinking and made it feel like a celebration. In my mind, avoiding alcohol during pregnancy proved I didn't have a problem, and I joked about those first postpartum drinks as a deserved reward for having healthy babies. Seeing other mothers resume drinking gave me added justification—if others could, why not me? Underneath, though, these rationalizations reflected a mix of wanting to fit in and the emotional urge to relieve stress. The pattern revealed my attempts to cope and my fluctuating feelings about alcohol's place in my life.

Avoiding alcohol during my pregnancies came easily. As soon as I learned I was expecting, I stopped drinking without struggle, craving, or temptation. I didn't feel left out or desire alcohol. The only time sobriety became difficult was after giving birth. What had been effortless before now felt impossible—quitting post-pregnancy wasn't straightforward. Picking up alcohol again, after months sober, felt like a personal failure, making me question my strength and emotional resilience. The contrast between easy sobriety during pregnancy and ongoing struggle afterward revealed a deeper emotional conflict I hadn't anticipated. I wondered why my emotional needs changed so drastically at different points in my journey.

While in active addiction, I didn't need something tragic to happen, and there didn't have to be something catastrophic setting me off to want to pick up a drink. It could just have been a cloudy day, someone could've cut me off, or not said thank you when I held the door, the dog was barking too much, the TV was too loud, or my husband didn't coddle me with the anticipated amount of attention and affection I desired before he left for work. I blamed everyone but myself for my own actions and thoughts, rarely owning them and acknowledging the consequences that lay before me.

I wanted my marriage to be perfect, but it wasn't. It still isn't. I pictured motherhood as always beautiful and light, filled with laughter and precious moments, yet reality never lived up to that. Achievements in others' eyes defined my success, though I'd never asked what it meant to me. If accolades rolled in from others, I was satisfied. I longed for a flawless, floating-on-cloud-nine life, but unsurprisingly, that hasn't happened. Falling short in those areas—when my story didn't match my imagined narrative—left me feeling like a failure: undeserving, unseen. It seemed easier, more comfortable, to give up. Give up on myself, on my marriage, on motherhood. If people already saw me as a nobody, making myself invisible felt inevitable.

Motherhood didn't create my drinking problem; it just

amplified what was already there. It shed light on the sadness. It heightened the madness. Periods of moderation made me think it wasn't so alarming. What once seemed like harmless fun became terrifying once I was responsible for a baby. Suddenly, the stakes were higher. I wasn't just hurting myself anymore. I wasn't just caring for myself; my priorities needed shifting. I was shaping my children's first memories, sometimes even risking their livelihoods. That realization hit hard. I had to look back and face the truth before I could even think about moving forward. I had to accept responsibility and hold myself accountable for my actions. That can be a tough pill to swallow. I had to look in the rear-view mirror and question myself and my actions on a daily basis.

I now know that life is full of triggers, and how I react is solely my decision. I can't control what happens, but I can control my response. I step away before overstimulation, care for myself when I feel too low, and ask for help before I spiral. Physically and emotionally, I recognize my triggers and no longer feel pulled to drink; instead, I feel drawn towards healing and being present. Now, I ask not why things happen to me, but how I can handle them more healthily.

Let these chapters be a support system for you, just as writing them has been for me. Let's cheer each other on, hold ourselves accountable, and celebrate every win, big and small, knowing there will be dozens of smalls before the bigs. Changing parts of who we are, altering our current versions and how we operate, isn't easy, but we always have the power to choose sobriety. That is something no one can take away from us, and that's a pretty powerful thing. The chance to build a better life for ourselves and our families is out there. We just have to believe we are strong enough to reach it and that *we deserve it.*

Want that life—want it with everything we have. Then take the first step, and don't stop. The rest of our story is waiting.

Part One: The Devil's Drug

"My birthing experience was traumatizing. I started

drinking immediately when I got home from the

hospital just to cope with my feelings."

–Rachel G., mother of two, sober 16 months

With my first baby, I was unexpectedly admitted for severe

preeclampsia at 37 weeks. I remember sitting in the Labor

& Delivery lobby for what I thought would be just a blood

pressure check-up, then calling Peter to let him know I'd be

on my way home. Once I was thoroughly examined, it was

decided that I needed to be induced immediately. I made yet

another phone call to Peter to say that instead of coming

home, he needed to grab our bags and head to the hospital. It

was go time. I waited for his arrival, terrified out of my mind for millions of reasons, trying to keep myself calm so as not to raise my blood pressure even further.

I had made a birth plan that I was confident in and hoped for a peaceful and calm experience from beginning to end. I envisioned breathing through contractions while holding Peter's hand after he finished rubbing my feet and feeding me ice chips. The room would be dim, with spa-like music playing. Perhaps there'd be some aromatherapy and one of those bouncy balls I'd have a go at. Maybe I'd walk the hospital halls, and people would say things like, "Congratulations, you must be so excited! It won't be long now!" I'd dab on some blush and slap on a quick coat of mascara, then push for approximately 8 minutes and have the nurse take an Instagram-worthy photo immediately after delivery, with the baby on my chest and Peter smiling off to the side. I would look tired yet fresh and vibrant at the same time, my new little family so happy and content, and I would glow from becoming a first-time mother; I wouldn't even need a highlighter and setting spray. I would then get some sleep while Peter rocked our sweet girl, and then we'd all go home together the next day. Overwhelmed with love and gratitude, excited for this new chapter ahead.

That's not how it went down. Not even close.

I was rushed and admitted from Labor and Delivery to a private room, where a doctor started talking about a Magnesium drip to get my blood pressure under control since the medication given in the emergency room wasn't effective in lowering it as they had anticipated. It was dangerously high and potentially fatal if not immediately tended to. If you've never been in labor with Magnesium, let me just say: you're lucky, it's brutal. A PTSD-worthy experience. My body was on fire from the inside out the moment it hit my veins. Nausea immediately came in waves, and I was certain I would throw up. I begged the nurse for a cold washcloth, convinced I wasn't going to make it through the next minute, while the doctor chirped on about God-knows-what. He could clearly see that I was in no position to receive any important information, so I assumed he would wait until Peter arrived to communicate what was happening, but nope, he kept on talking. I can't remember his name, what he looked like, or anything he said—it was all a blur.

Being on a Magnesium drip is like being drunk—blurry vision, slurred speech, barely able to move my limbs, and unable to focus my eyes. The room was spinning, and voices were echoing through my head each time someone spoke. I felt helpless. I felt angry that this was my experience and sad that none of what I wanted it to be was actually what it was. My labor was quickly started with Pitocin and a Foley balloon—also awful. *If you know, you know.* Then, thanks to a rare blood-clotting lab test, the delivery team paused everything, worried about the potential of excessive bleeding. I begged God to let it be over, one way or another, while we waited over 12 hours for the test results. The next morning, Pitocin was started back up again. I was induced **twice**, and on Magnesium the entire time. They only turned the Mag off while I pushed after I had begged and pleaded with them not to make me meet my baby on that devil of a drug. The moment she was out, they flipped it right back on. I spent five days in that hospital bed, unable to hold my daughter without assistance or get up on my own. I couldn't safely walk to the restroom, so I was cathed and couldn't eat the entire time I was in labor, so I was now starving as well. What should have been a beautiful moment turned into a nightmare. Even now—on Piper's birthday or Mother's Day or even when the topic of childbirth arises—I get that feeling in the pit of my stomach that takes me back to those moments. I don't think Peter even realizes how truly traumatizing it all was for me and how, even all these years later, I still think about it.

My postpartum depression kicked into high gear before I even left the hospital on that fifth day. I was traumatized and in shock the first few days after giving birth. I remember bringing Piper home to meet my mother, who was excitedly waiting for us, and then crying alone in the basement stairwell as soon as we walked through the door. The countertop was already crowded with bottles and pacifiers, freshly sanitized. The house suddenly felt smaller than when I was last in it. Sliding towards a new low, letting myself fall even further, honestly felt easier than stopping, and those early moments were just the beginning. What a tough way to start out motherhood, huh? Nothing as I had anticipated, that's for sure. I wasn't resting easy back at home and getting the hang of things. I was in survival mode from day one.

People on the outside, especially those who had no idea what I had just gone through, expected me to bounce back physically, mentally, and emotionally, but inside, I was desperately searching for any piece of the person I used to be before all of this happened. I began to wonder if I ever even really knew her. What was she like? What made her special? If she showed up today, would I even recognize her? Would I want to? Who was I becoming, and do I like that person? We often don't even notice the changes or transitions until they're final. It's something we all wrestle with as life ebbs and flows. Priorities shift, and you are simply no longer who you used to be, especially when you become a parent and your entire world changes.

I loved my child fiercely, but is it okay to want a break, to want something for just myself again? Overstimulation set in, and suddenly, I was touched out—checked out. In those early months, I was just trying to survive in the trenches with limited contact with the outside world. My days and nights revolved around sleep schedules, naps, feedings, tummy time, and wake windows. Meanwhile, the pressure to always be "grateful" just piled on more guilt.

I wanted to be the champion of it all and not only rock at being a new mother but also keep my house spotless and have a social life. I wanted to take my baby with me everywhere and show her off. I wanted to sleep like a normal person and have time to shower and get dressed—maybe even put on some makeup.

Why could other mothers do that, but I couldn't? Why was it so hard for me, and why did I feel so sorry for myself?

Let's Reflect

1. What version of yourself did you assume would show up when you became a mother?

2. What fears did you have about losing your independence, identity, or control?

3. Which expectations of motherhood came from you, and which were handed to you by others?

4. If you could whisper one truth to your "pre-motherhood" self, what would it be?

Let's Affirm It

You're still in there; you just have to find yourself. You're not lost, you're busy searching for your truth.

Say it with me now – "I am not lost."

Statistically Speaking

Nearly **1 in 5** women experience postpartum depression or anxiety, but fewer than half ever disclose it to a healthcare professional. (Source: CDC, 2024 Maternal Mental Health Report)

Part Two: Living the Dream

"Couldn't stop the baby from crying? Drink. Finally got her to stop crying? Drink. I'm exhausted? Drink. Got three consecutive hours of sleep? Drink. I wish I could say I caught on quickly—that I realized how far I'd fallen before things got really dark. But I didn't. I kept convincing myself I was fine, that maybe every mom felt this way, that I deserved a break. That this was just my new normal. But eventually, I had to face the truth: alcohol was taking more from me than it was giving. I had to do the work from the ground up and accept that postpartum is real—and when mixed with alcohol, it's dangerous."

–Danielle Lawrence, mother of two, sober 20 months

The frayed edges of a baby blanket, piled in a heap, lay on the kitchen floor amongst crumbs and spilled milk—a snapshot of the chaos that is motherhood. I've always cringed at the obvious comments, like, "Wow, you've got your hands full." Of course I do. Of course WE do. Parenting is tough at any age, but toddlers take it to a whole new level. To be real, motherhood is the hardest job I've ever had. Every stage comes with its own hurdles and victories. Sometimes, those hurdles feel impossible, with the fear of failure always lurking.

Trust me, mothers don't need reminders about how overwhelmed or exhausted we look. We live and breathe twenty-four seven for our kids, always putting their needs first. That's the job, right? Once the baby comes home, so does the psychological load that the mother bears. It's more than sleepless nights and endless chores—it's the mental checklist that never shuts off: doctor's appointments, playdates, meal planning, remembering every little thing for everyone else. From birth, through toddlerhood, into the next phase, there's always some new challenge or behavior to work through.

We as mothers become the invisible engine that keeps the family running—the heartbeat of the home. But no matter how much we do or how hard we try, there's always more waiting. The load is constant, and sometimes it feels like we're carrying it all alone. Honestly, more often than not, we are.

Even when surrounded by people, motherhood can feel incredibly lonely and isolating. That's something no mother wants to admit: the silent, invisible work that never ends. Always feeling out of the loop when it comes to what's going on around us socially or in society. Being in a room full of people and feeling the most alone one has ever felt. Life and everyone else are buzzing by while you—the mother—are standing still, struggling to keep up. No longer noticing the beautiful sunny days or the flowers blooming in the front yard, but now seeing the flowers as just another job to tend to, and the sun as an added inconvenience, requiring sunscreen and hats for the kids to go outside. The joy in the little things gets lost, displaced if you will, and it becomes an afterthought behind the chore. The slightest touch from a partner feels like pins and needles on already overstimulated skin, the noises of the world wreaking havoc on your nervous system. Talk about dysregulation. Having friends all call and text to check in, yet feeling like no one cares or understands what is happening. Mad and sad all at once, tears of anger, resentment, and hopelessness often pool in the eyes.

As these challenges piled up, I realized just how much

motherhood would test me. Looking back, I see how much this new chapter rocked me to my core. It flipped me upside down and shook me until I felt like a rag doll. No matter how hard I tried or attempted to get myself on the right track, to find a different perspective, to hold myself with some grace—I couldn't do it. I wanted to, but I couldn't.

Don't get me wrong, I never thought parenting would be a walk in the park, I'm not that naive. But I didn't expect it to hit *this* hard. The triggers. The emotions. I had no clue I'd struggle so much inside my own head or feel trapped by my own thoughts. Negative thinking and intrusive thoughts became my unwanted guest and closest companion, always working their way into my psyche. I have a history of anxiety and depression, so I tried to brace myself for what was coming before the storm had even hit. I educated myself on the effects of the rapidly changing hormones and spoke to friends who had children to gain some knowledge and advice from their experiences. I had heard about the 'baby blues,' but I didn't really understand what that meant until I had it. The term 'baby blues' is complete bullshit and gets tossed around so nonchalantly that it makes it seem like it just whispers by you, barely recognizable. It's not the blues, it's the blackest

of blacks. It's the darkest, worst possible mental space one

can live in, and it happens to way more women than you can

imagine. There's nothing cutesy about it, and it's not as short-

lived as professionals may make it out to be. The questionnaire

I had to fill out at my first and only postpartum appointment

was a joke. There's no possible way six questions could

accurately capture what I was feeling just weeks after delivery.

There's no way the three minutes spent talking about how I

was feeling was enough time to cover the realness of what was

happening to me. Why aren't we being asked more in-depth

questions? What I needed then was a moment of true empathy

and understanding, a simple acknowledgment that my pains

and fears were real, and a guiding hand showing me the way

forward. Why doesn't it feel like the doctors who are with us

through the nine months of pregnancy care about our mental

and emotional well-being now that the baby has arrived? Is

society really that blind to how dramatically damaging it can

be to a mother to suffer through these thoughts and emotions

basically alone?

People (including society and other mothers) don't talk

enough about the emotional fallout of first-time motherhood. The intrusive thoughts, the mood swings, the tears—on a wild ride full of rage that you want to get off but can't, and it's so much more than just being tired. Bit by bit, you lose pieces of yourself. I'd look in the mirror and barely recognize the woman staring back, especially after another sleepless night or meltdown. That feeling that you could possibly just die from lack of sleep is a real thing. I remember many days when I genuinely had no idea how I was going to make it through the day. And on top of that, I'm supposed to be being productive with my child, teaching them something new, not worrying about milestones and leaps and learning colors and shapes while limiting TV time? Sure.

Days blurred together, one tumbling into the next. The simple routines that used to make me feel like "me"—my hobbies, my work, my writing, even just time alone to go to the bathroom—vanished. I used to get ready in the quiet stillness of the house, run errands on my own, and have uninterrupted phone calls. Now, I didn't know who I was anymore. Just a mother? Maybe. But surely not the woman I used to be—whoever that was. My identity was tangled in the despair, knotted so tightly that I just wanted to feel like myself again, but I carried myself with frustration because I couldn't remember anything about what made me, me.

Sleep is broken, if it comes at all. Every conversation gets interrupted, and even the simplest task feels huge. Every day is a new test, and sometimes just surviving the next hour is a win. Those early days blurred together, and before you know it, you've morphed into a new version of yourself— sometimes without even realizing it. As I struggled to settle into my new role, the pressure kept building. I felt I was expected to always know what to do, but really, I was just making it up as I went along. The expectation to be the perfect mother was always there, judging every stumble. I constantly compared myself to other mothers, as if it were a competition. I set all these strict parenting rules for myself—breastfeeding only, serving only homemade baby food, not allowing screentime—but when reality hit, and I switched to formula or let Ms. Rachel help out, I felt like I'd failed. The truth is, I set myself up for judgment before anyone else even got the chance.

How do other mothers make it look so easy? What am I missing? How did I mess it up so quickly? My mental health took a nosedive. No matter what anyone says, being a stay-at-home mom is hands down the hardest job out there. Nothing compares to being needed around the clock with no breaks, no pay, and no finish line. I convinced myself that, because I wasn't a perfect mother, I was a terrible one, and that life would always be this hard. I wasn't sure I'd ever be happy again. Maybe I never really was that happy to begin with. Leaving my job to stay home felt like the right choice at the time, but not now. Working outside of the home gave me a sense of purpose, it gave me something to focus on outside of motherhood, and allowed me a creative outlet. As my daughter grew, so did the overwhelming anxiety of day-to-day life. Privacy disappeared. Freedom vanished. Even a quick coffee run was out of reach. I felt trapped in my own home, desperate for someone to save me from this mental and emotional storm—but no one was coming. Isn't this what I wanted?

Isn't this the dream?

There weren't many things that brought relief in those first months of motherhood. I shut myself off from friends and family, not wanting to burden them with my depression and anxiety. Feeling like they just wouldn't understand, and embarrassed that I was still struggling so deeply. I just didn't have the energy to keep up with life like I once did. Once I stopped breastfeeding after about three months (thanks to my daughter's milk allergy), I didn't see any harm in having a glass of wine to unwind. *She's on formula now, so what's the risk?* Honestly, it worked. It was instant gratification and worked immediately, something I was grateful for. For a while, a glass or two at night really did take the edge off. The heaviness in my chest would lighten, and the chaos felt more manageable. But on the harder days, one glass wasn't enough, so it turned into two, then three. As my little one grew from newborn to infant to toddler, my habit grew with it. My tolerance shot up, and I just kept pouring without a second thought, desperate to keep up with the only thing that I felt like made me feel better.

Slowly, the wine started flowing earlier and earlier in the day—first in the mid-afternoon around nap time, then at lunch, and eventually even at breakfast, until it replaced my morning coffee. I'd wait for my husband to leave for work so I could pour my first glass. Anxious for him to go so I could get my fix and stop feeling so fidgety. Once I started drinking during the day, going back to moderation wasn't even on the table. I had established a new routine, fitting alcohol in it seamlessly. I felt impossibly stuck. I didn't want to be a stay-at-home mom anymore, but I also didn't want to leave Piper with anyone else or send her to daycare. I knew how blessed I was to be able to stay home with her and get that time with her, but what good is it if I can't even remember most days anyway? I complained to Peter about how stressed out I was, but the idea of going back to work meant losing the tiny sliver of freedom I still had, which, honestly, was just the ability to drink whenever I wanted. If I were at work, I couldn't drink, and I wasn't ready to give that up. At home, I could always DoorDash some champagne for my mimosas, run to the corner store, and lazily drink the day away. If I were under no pressure to make a change, why would I?

I reached a time when I packed the diaper bag with the precision of a medic under fire. Wipes? Check. Extra clothes? Check. Snacks, sunscreen, and toys? Check. And tucked between the diapers and Desitin… a mini bottle of rosé, just in case I needed to take the edge off after library story time. I didn't have a drinking problem—I had a coping strategy. This was how I made it through the day, and that's all that mattered to me.

Mothers don't get to clock out, so we find ways to blur the edges. For me, it came chilled and in a bottle. It wasn't just about the alcohol—it was about having *one thing* in the bag that was just for me. A secret comfort in a world where I was everything to everyone and nothing to myself. I needed something to latch onto that made me feel better, regardless of its negative effects on my life, relationships, and health.

I didn't feel guilty—just constantly exhausted, and I wondered if this was what motherhood was supposed to feel like: always waiting for the day things would *feel* different. Maybe not everyone was making the same choices or feeling similar pains. Maybe there was another way, and I just wasn't seeing it. Maybe I wasn't deserving of that relief and ease. Most of my close friends had young kids too, but as far as I knew, they weren't sipping Sauvignon Blanc in the preschool pickup line. And if I did know that, would I judge them?

There's a longing within all of us to feel like we are a part of something. We often bend and flex ourselves to fit that narrative of what we think is perfect and what we think is normal. Society says look here, click here, and we won't judge you, we're all on the same team. At that time, I liked having something to fall into, not having to make too many decisions for myself.

I found myself constantly reaching for my phone whenever I had a quiet moment, but this behavior became a crutch and a safety blanket that didn't make me feel safe; it made me feel sad. I tossed and turned in bed at night, my thoughts doing the same. Unable to sleep for dozens of reasons, the alcohol being one of them. I ruminated on how other mothers had it all together, playing the imposter syndrome game and shaming myself for everything I did and didn't do throughout the day. It made me mad to see that other mothers didn't have the same struggles. How do they make it look so easy? How are their days so productive and seamless? How is their house so damn quiet and clean?! How are they doing it all and still indulging in brunch with friends, and where the hell did they find these friends? When did they have the time or energy to get their house so clean? Where did they find these husbands that moonlight as Prince Charming's, and how did they still look so fresh and rested while doing it all? Surely, I was missing the mark and doing something wrong since my life didn't look like theirs. I wasted so many hours mad about how easy and perfect their lives seemed. I'd look at them, then at myself—stretch-marked, unshowered, barely holding it together. I lived on dry shampoo and a prayer most days; skin care routines and makeup hauls were far from what I had to work with.

What the hell is wrong with me? Why can they do this, and I can't?

And woven right there, between the meal-prep reels and curated nurseries, the romantic gestures from their husbands and perfect, sleep-trained babies was the solution the internet handed to me: wine. The internet promoted and pushed it, encouraged it, really. Branded it and glamorized it. New drinks were released specifically targeted at mothers, making it seem silly for us not to partake. There was an entire culture that left the impression of wine making motherhood more manageable and the mothers more interesting, more fun.

It isn't subtle; it is everywhere—on mugs, t-shirts, memes, store ads and end caps, Facebook, and Instagram. "Mommy needs wine." "It's wine o'clock." "Pour yourself a glass—you survived the day." It is in Etsy shops, Target, TikTok, and in mom groups. It is marketed not as an addiction, but as lighthearted, harmless "self-care." Suburban alcoholism at its finest, presented as a solution and not a threat. It's just moms having fun, right? It's become a community of mothers looking for others to justify, glamorize, and make the act feel more acceptable—playfully joking and dancing around the dangers.

Honestly, the validation felt *so* good. Wine culture let me admit motherhood was exhausting without actually saying it out loud. The sarcasm in every meme reassured me that, of course, this is overwhelming and not for the weak. *Pour yourself a drink; you've earned it.* And for a while, that worked. Wine culture dulled the chaos and gave me something that was just mine when everything else was being consumed by others.

But here's the thing about mommy wine culture: it's sneaky as hell. It shows up in pastel colors with fancy fonts and cheeky dish towels. It's baked into book clubs, playdates, and every group chat where someone says, "OMG, I need a drink after today." It feels harmless, even funny—until the punchline becomes your reality. Until the joke stops being funny because drinking is how you survive. You're no longer cute with a cocktail; you're the stigma and statistic.

That was me. And I wasn't laughing anymore.

I joined multiple online mom groups, desperate for

connection, craving mom friends, and someone to talk to other than my husband or my own mother to tell me I wasn't failing and that I was doing a good job. To tell me I was a part of this elite group of individuals. Instead, I found rules, competition, and the occasional ban when I pushed back. Groups that are positioned to be helpful, inclusive, and supportive now felt threatening and judgmental. I muted the online mom group notifications while convincing myself I belonged to some secret club of women who "got it." Except belonging shouldn't require hiding. It requires being seen. And I wasn't. My invisibility hung like a cloak, heavy and hearty. I felt worse about myself while in most of these mom groups than I did before I joined them. Self-doubt, intrusive thoughts, and scrutiny all became core parts of my psyche.

Has anyone else ever rage-unfollowed a mom influencer after realizing they just spent an hour staring at her spotless living room, perfectly hung family photos, and flawless makeup while everything about you, your life, and your space was a train wreck? We're all guilty of the comparison game, and I told myself if they could drink and still be good moms, so could I. But I genuinely couldn't. I was the mom snapping at my kid for knocking over my wine glass, running out to the car during dance class for a quick swig, hiding in the bathroom with a glass of rosé, and chugging champagne out of coffee mugs on the way to the bank. I'll be the first to say it: I wasn't a good mom. I was the worst version of myself, and I knew it. I was a fraud. I got so good at pretending to be okay, convincing myself that my actions were justified – the queen of making excuses, if you will. According to a 2020 study, 55% of mothers reported feeling pressured by social media to maintain an unrealistic image of their lives, with a significant number admitting to concealing their struggles with alcohol as part of this facade. I painted the facade of having a perfect life to everyone on the outside looking in, but that couldn't be further from reality.

Motherhood is isolating enough without addiction. I was already isolated enough and longing for someone to swoop in and save me from myself. The loneliness was deafening and defeating me day in and day out. I was an addict by definition but not by declaration. Moms aren't supposed to take mugshots; we're supposed to get flu shots. Moms don't do DUIs; we do ABCs. We don't do court dates; we do play dates. Those addict stigmas just don't complement us, so we refuse to wear them even when they're staring us right in the face. With empty eyes and clouded minds, we go through the motions, aware of what the fallout may bring but also blindly playing with fire.

Addiction doesn't always mean probation and a record—sometimes it's just a mom going through the motions, physically there but mentally checked out. Smiling on the outside, counting down to bedtime—and that glass. Eyes empty, mind foggy, on the edge.

And the worst part? I believed this was normal. *Just a glass to take the edge off. Everyone does it. You're fine.* Except I wasn't fine. I was lying to myself more convincingly than I lied to anyone else.

I wasn't just buying wine—I was buying into the belief that I could numb myself and still be a good mother. That alcohol wasn't the problem, but the solution. That drinking would stay cute, funny, and relatable.

It didn't stay cute.

As my tolerance climbed, I started slipping. I wasn't hiding my dependency as well as I had thought. Peter noticed the decline in both my health and behavior that quickly roller-coastered us to hell. We began fighting even more, which I didn't think was possible, and he picked up on the slight ticks that, if you will, shone a light on what I was doing in the dark. Skipping out to the store when we didn't really need anything, making excuses to leave the house at the most inopportune times, and always being prone to a fickle mood. Still, I prided myself on seeming composed, but really, I was just sinking deeper into addiction.

I kept excusing myself to run for groceries, even though I really just needed a refill. I scrolled past "mommy needs wine" memes while sipping champagne at 8 a.m., thinking, *Exactly, Mommy does.* And whenever my daughter pointed at my glass and asked for a sip of "Mommy's juice," I laughed it off. But inside, I knew. Kids, with all their innocence, expose the problem for you without even trying.

I kept telling myself I was surviving. But really, I was disappearing.

If I'm honest, my relationship with alcohol started way before motherhood. Long before babies, there were barstools. Happy hours turned into closing time, first dates drowned in cocktails, and brunches where mimosas flowed faster than coffee. I was always game to go out, the girl who could keep up with the guys—or outdrink them. I knew the bartenders by name, could take a shot with confidence (even if I threw it up later). Drinking became part of my identity, my social shield. I desperately wanted to belong, to have friends who were excited to see me. I honestly believed alcohol would make me that girl everyone loved, not realizing what it was really doing to my relationships.

Back then, it didn't feel like a problem. It felt like freedom—just part of growing up when everyone around you drank, too. Alcohol softened my restless mind, blurred the edges of insecurity, and made the world feel easier, at least for a little while. I drank to celebrate, to numb, even just because it was Tuesday. It was a way to drown out the self-doubt and constant noise in my head.

Before motherhood, alcohol showed up everywhere—woven through every friendship, party, breakup, milestone—almost every day of my life. It was my plus-one and my constant companion. It helped me feel confident, sexy, funny, and bold. But looking back, I see it also kept me from truly knowing myself or letting others know me. It numbed the pain, sure, but it also dulled my joy and became my mask. I missed out on fully feeling things—raw, real, open, and honest. Like many of us, I'm not proud of a lot of my past. Sometimes I forget the worst parts of it, or I block out experiences, because reliving them feels uncomfortable or embarrassing. I fell victim to sexual abuse as a child by a family member and never told anyone until late into adulthood. I didn't dare speak of it because I felt that I had not earned the title of victim since the abuse wasn't "that bad," and never thought anyone would believe me anyway. As a young and impressionable 8-year-old girl, the abuse had a severe effect on my adult relationships with men and could have potentially acted as a catalyst for my addiction.

In my twenties and early 30s, it almost felt glamorous. Hangovers were badges, wild weekends made for good stories. In LA, there was always another party, another club, another celebrity sighting. But underneath, things were cracking. Missed alarms, missed deadlines, apologies muttered through a dry mouth and bloodshot eyes. I kept up the act—smoothed things over, cleaned up well—but deep down, I knew this wasn't sustainable. My subconscious was already warning me.

In our early twenties and thirties, heavy drinking felt normal—everyone did it on weekends, and Sunday Funday just meant nursing hangovers and keeping the party going. Mimosas and Bloody Marys flowed like it was always Friday night, even with work looming on Monday. Friends cheered each other on, held hair back, and swapped stories. Even though my dad was an alcoholic, I never labeled myself that way. I told myself there was no way I'd end up like him, losing control to a bottle. I thought it was ridiculous that anyone couldn't just stop drinking. I kept bingeing because I believed I was still in control.

My addictions started early, be it shoplifting at the mall as a young teen who was desperate for their mother's attention, falling in love with a handsome drug dealer who put me in dangerous situations, wrecked my credit, and got us evicted, or stealing from complete strangers by breaking into cars. It was the way my cocaine addiction led me to sleep in my car or a random stranger's house for several months during my twenties. It dropped me off at crack houses in the nicest suburbs, unsuspecting to the naked eye, but filled with addicts cooking crack in the kitchen, and I sleeping on the floor of an empty bedroom with a black trash bag full of my belongings. It was escaping from real danger—dealers pointing guns at my car as I sped off from a deal gone bad, using fake money to buy drugs. Looking back, it's hard to believe I was ever that reckless and that that was literally my life. But here I am, trying to make sense of it all. Trying to find a reason within it and move on.

So, when motherhood came crashing in, it wasn't just the sleepless nights, the crying, or the isolation that broke me. It was realizing I had built my whole adult life around a vision of a future that didn't work with the kind of mom I wanted to be—whatever that meant. Worse, I had no idea who I was without it, and that scared the shit out of me.

There's always a settling-in period once you bring a baby home, where you feel so lost and like you have absolutely no clue what you're doing. I remember at one point thinking to myself, "They let me just walk out of the hospital with a baby —what do I do now?" You walk through your front door, and suddenly everything is different, but nothing around you has changed—another parallel with rehab, and that parallel is wild. The rooms look the same, but the energy is off-kilter. Every object seems to have a new purpose—safety checked, baby-proofed, or moved out of the way.

Looking back at those first few months, I recognize how strong I really am. Strength, coincidentally, is the most necessary part of sobriety. As an addict, though, you must choose which direction you point that strength. Are you going up with it or down? What we, as mothers, are capable of is truly astounding and life-changing, from the inside out.

Let's Reflect

1. What moments made you realize you were no longer drinking for fun, but to function?

2. How did alcohol (or another escape) become a friend, then a captor?

3. What lies did you tell yourself to make it all seem okay?

4. What parts of you were you trying to silence when you poured that next glass?

5. When you think about "rock bottom," what scares you more —the fall, or what you'll have to face without the escape?

Let's Affirm It

The truth won't kill you. The pretending might.

Statistically Speaking

Roughly 1 in 10 mothers report drinking alcohol daily by their child's first birthday, and 1 in 5 admit to using alcohol to "cope with parenting stress." (Source: National Institute on Alcohol Abuse and Alcoholism, 2024)

Part Three: Doom Scrolling

"My drinking had gotten out of control, and I was ready to stop.

NA drinks have been a huge component of my sobriety. They are

like (major) harm reduction for me when I have a craving."

–Lindsey J., mother of one, sober 14 months

Here's what I see now: mommy wine culture wasn't just

a joke—it was a business plan. Alcohol companies were

fully aware of the consequences they pushed with their

marketing. In the early 2000s, wine was rebranded not as an

indulgence, but as a lifestyle accessory. Aesthetic. Relatable.

Instagrammable. And who was the prime target? Women.

More specifically, *mothers.*

Because here's the thing: we're vulnerable. We're exhausted,

isolated, and desperate for relief. We're starved for connection and validation. We're drowning in invisible labor. And what better way to sell us a coping mechanism than to disguise it as a community?

The wine wear. The novelty stemless glasses. The "mommy juice" shirts. They weren't harmless jokes—they were straight-up advertising. Normalizing. Grooming us to believe alcohol wasn't a problem, it was the solution to all of our problems.

And it worked. A 2020 study found women's alcohol consumption jumped by 41% during the pandemic. That's not a coincidence—that's targeted marketing, capitalism feeding on our exhaustion. Realizing my disease was profitable for someone else made me furious.

Now in recovery, I see social media differently. I curate my feed like my sobriety depends on it—because sometimes, it does— sober moms, recovery pages, real talk only. And when I catch myself sliding back into old habits, I pause. Breathe. Log off. Unfollow and unfriend. Because the truth is, nobody's life is as perfect as it looks online. And none of us are as alone as we think.

In treatment, I realized how deep the conditioning went.

How normalized it had become to medicate motherhood or any life-changing event, really, with alcohol. How capitalism and culture were profiting off of mothers numbing themselves into oblivion, making it their business. And how, underneath the memes and merch, was an entire generation of women quietly drowning.

I still laugh at a good wine meme—but I see the truth under the punchline: exhaustion, loneliness, the ache to feel seen. I remind myself: I don't need to drink to belong or to survive. I hold the power to choose my direction, not a glass.

Here's the other thing about mommy wine culture: it's sneaky as hell. It shows up covered in sarcasm. It's baked into book clubs and park playdates and every group chat where someone says, "OMG, I need a drink after today." And it's all fun and games until you start realizing your "fun" is the only thing getting you through the day—and you're not really laughing anymore. You're miserable and self-loathing. It's a lot easier to feel sorry for yourself when your mind is switched into survival mode. Once one foot's in the door of doom, forget it, you're going to fall in.

Here's the truth: wine culture sells a fantasy. It promises

that drinking will make you funnier, prettier, more relaxed, and a better mom. But it's a scam. You're not sexier drunk or more interesting—just quieter in your own head while your actions shout, "Pay attention to me!" The price for that silence is yourself.

Motherhood didn't create my addiction—it just turned up the volume on what was already there. Motherhood gave me clarity: if I kept going, I wasn't just losing myself. I was losing my daughters and the family I'd always wanted.

And that realization was the thing no one could make funny.

Even as I rolled my eyes at the world around me, I saw the real need underneath. Moms are craving validation, advice, and survival tips. Under it all, that relentless wine culture drumbeat: mommy needs wine, pour a glass, take the edge off. I jumped on that train and pulled others with me. It dulled the noise—until it didn't.

I kept showing up for my kids, doing what needed to be done, but I wasn't really present. It was like I was watching my own life from the outside, going through the motions, counting down the hours until bedtime—and that glass. I thought I had everyone fooled, but the truth is, none of us are really hiding it as well as we think we are. You're not alone, mama. So many of us have walked this path and felt the heavy weight of isolation. Reaching out is how we start to find our way back to ourselves.

I was constantly mad at myself. If it was so easy to immediately stop drinking when I was pregnant, why was it so hard when I wasn't pregnant? Do you tell yourself that next week will be different, come Monday, things are going to change? Or how about tomorrow you won't drink, at least not during the day. Maybe you convince yourself you can cut down, and your "problem" really isn't a problem.

You do realize that's complete bullshit, right?

I was the girl with so much promise. That's what my teachers said. That's what relatives whispered. That's what I told myself late at night, when the world was quiet, and the buzz wore off, and I was left alone with my thoughts. I was going to do something big. I was going to live loudly, bravely, brilliantly. And then, little by little, I handed that girl over to a glass, a bottle, a night out, a morning after. The ambition faded into the background, replaced by plans that revolved around the next drink, the next party, the next escape.

The most devastating part isn't even the lost opportuni-ties—it's the erosion of self-trust. The way you start breaking promises to yourself so casually, you almost don't notice. The way you become two people: the one everyone sees and the one you carry inside, bruised and stumbling and gasping for air. I lied to myself more skillfully than I lied to anyone else, convincing myself that I was fine, I was fun, I was functioning.

The truth is, I wasn't fine. I was numbing. I was grieving a version of myself I didn't know how to become. And the tragedy is, the people around me—some of them saw, some of them didn't, but none of them could pull me out. That was work only I could do.

I look back now and wonder: what could have been different? Could one conversation, one intervention, one honest moment have changed the course? Or was this always the road I had to walk to get here, to this reckoning, to this raw, trembling place where I finally call the thing by its name?

I don't have the answer. But I know this: what addiction took from me was real, but what I build in its place will be real, too. And maybe—just maybe—that's where the redemption begins.

Quitting wasn't a lightning bolt moment. It was a slow burn, growing hotter and harder to ignore until I either jumped out of the fire or got burned to ash.

I started to ask myself the hard questions.

Why do I need this?

What am I trying not to feel?

Who am I without alcohol?

I didn't love the answers. But I kept asking.

And let me tell you—early sobriety with toddlers is its own kind of hell. There's no numbing, no buffer. You're raw, exposed, and fully present for every tantrum, every mess, every irrational sippy cup meltdown. Some days, I felt like my skin was inside-out.

But you know what else happened?

I started to really feel again—the good, the bad, the everyday stuff. I laughed harder, cried more honestly, and even yelled a little less (well, sometimes). I showed up in ways that scared me, because I couldn't hide anymore.

We're powerless over alcohol. If you're reading this, you probably know that too. That's the first step in AA, and whether or not you're into meetings, it's true. AA and Sober

Mom groups can be helpful, but they can also get cliquey or preachy. Here's the honest truth: no group, affirmation, or meeting can keep you sober. Only you can do that. And there's more power in that than you think.

It's true that having support helps—people who lift you up, cheer you on, and don't enable you. But it's not mandatory. If you rely solely on others to keep you sober, it's not realistic. No one can hold your hand every moment or be there right when you're triggered. Mandatory meetings in treatment felt preachy to me. I'd tune out, doing word searches while rules and traditions were read because it was just too repetitive for me. The same sad song every single time just didn't resonate with me. If it does for you, then great, keep going. I personally don't like the idea of my sobriety being dependent on following steps that require me to make lists and apologize to people who have intentionally hurt me. Find my fault and part in being abused? Fuck off. That mentality can be dangerous, and I warn those in early sobriety to tread lightly through the steps if that's the route you've chosen.

I listened to everyone share their stories, their hope and desperation, their stumbles and wins. Don't get me wrong, it can be inspiring, but you don't have to be in the audience to find your own sobriety. After treatment, they suggested "90 in 90"—90 meetings in 90 days to all of us graduating from the program. That felt impossible for me. I didn't have the time as a stay-at-home mom, yet I was expected to make the time, or else I'd be labeled as someone who didn't take this seriously. That I wasn't ready for change, and my sobriety wasn't my priority. Again, bullshit.

I didn't connect with any meetings until I was 7 or 8 months sober, when I found a Sunday group of some younger women who were mainly moms. There, I felt seen and supported, even if we weren't lifelong friends. Sometimes you just need a place where you belong, even briefly.

But even in those circles, there were people who insisted, "If you think you can do this without AA, you're wrong." That always rubbed me the wrong way. No one else gets to define your success in recovery. On my one-year anniversary, I told that same group: "You don't need meetings to stay sober. You need strength and resilience from within." Everyone messes up—nearly every addict slips at some point. You can't promise you'll never drink again, and you shouldn't. There's no guarantee. Relapse happens, whether you're 20 months in or 20 years. What matters is that you keep coming back to yourself and the reasons you're doing this in the first place.

When you're in recovery, you're relearning how to live—one baby step at a time. Your mind needs time to reset and rest. All those brain pathways have to rewire after active addiction. For the first time in adulthood, you're facing life without a crutch. There's no numbing, just feeling everything and working through emotions in real time. The only way forward is honesty, without the mask of a drink.

It's hard. It's uncomfortable. But it's also worth it. Little by little, you start to feel alive again. You learn to sit with sadness rather than numb it, and you realize how strong you really are. People in recovery are some of the strongest people I know—the dedication it takes is no small thing. The reward, though, is worth it.

The feed never shows the moments that break us—only the ones we can filter.

Let's Reflect

1. What do you use social media for? (to get ideas, fashion + beauty advice, funny videos, etc.)

2. How often do you measure your worth against someone else's highlight reel?

3. If you could post the real image of your motherhood right now, what would it look like?

4. Is social media harming or helping your mental health?

5. If social media didn't exist, how would you scale up against other mothers?

Let's Affirm It

You don't owe the world a polished version of your pain. Say it with me now – I don't owe anyone, anything.

Statistically Speaking

64% of mothers report that social media makes them feel "inadequate" compared to other moms, and **42%** admit to posting content that doesn't reflect their real experience. (Source: Motherly State of Motherhood Report, 2024)

Part Four: Another Round

"Finally, after blackouts, not remembering who I was with or how I got home, I couldn't take the pain any longer. I admitted myself to a treatment center. I wanted my kids to see me sober."
–Connie Kay, mother of two, sober three years

After having my first daughter, things were already rough, and both my husband and I knew it. I knew what to expect with a second baby on the way—more hormonal sadness and anxiety, more sleepless nights, more chaos. But no amount of experience could have prepared me for round two of childbearing. I mentally braced myself as best I could for someone who was still struggling with postpartum depression from the first baby. I was in for a lot more emotions and a lot less sanity this go around, and I felt like a walking nervous breakdown. I knew I was going to feel like shit both mentally and emotionally.

My mother stayed with us for the first two months after my second daughter, Tilly, was born, and thank God she did—she truly went above and beyond despite having a front row seat to the shitshow. I wouldn't have survived without the help; I deeply believe that. Having a second baby brought a whole new level of emotional and practical upheaval. Postpartum depression once again convinced me I was a horrible mother and undeserving of even a glimmer of happiness. This wasn't just the "baby blues" again—this was a full-on storm. More rocky, treacherous, and damaging than the first one.

Piper struggled with having a newborn in the house a lot more than I expected. Suddenly, she had to share my attention, and she hated it—honestly, I think she still does. I felt so much guilt trying to stretch myself between both girls, each of them wanting Mom at the exact same time, all of the time. I couldn't find the balance and the beauty of the experience; I only felt the stress and saw the burdens that it brought.

That second round of postpartum depression really did me in; I truly stood no chance against it. As mothers, we harbor so much emotion and sensitivity within us, so that when we feel something, we really feel it, deep. I knew that after my second pregnancy, I had the opportunity to continue the alcohol abstinence I had maintained so easily during pregnancy. It was the perfect time to stay sober and allow my body the time it needed to heal and mend.

However, I picked up drinking again even sooner this time. I knew Peter was more aware of my habits and would call me out on it if he saw me drinking, so I tried harder to hide it. I hid bottles in dusty corners of the house. I stashed bottles and half-empty glasses in the most obscure places that I was certain no one would find. Sometimes I hid things so well I'd surprise myself, stumbling upon glasses I'd forgotten. Hiding became routine—just another layer of isolation.

I would hide bottles in the laundry room, behind the washer and dryer, or under the bathroom sink, behind the Clorox wipes. I was pouring champagne muffled under blankets in the basement so my husband wouldn't hear the pop of the bottle. The cracks in my life deepened as I hid bottles in the kids' rooms, in the Christmas storage bins, and even in the sock drawer. My heart would race as I retraced my steps through the house, trying to recall each and every glass from that day. *Did I check the cookie jar and behind the cat food? What about under the baby's dresser or in the diaper bag? Did I get the one stashed between my sweatshirts in my closet, or in my coat pockets? What about those mini bottles I shoved into the plant?* I got so good at hiding my drinks that two years sober, I still find empties, and it makes me feel physically ill.

This went on for most of Tilly's first year. The more I drank—about a bottle and a half of wine and champagne a day, the more I slipped. It was aggravating that I couldn't seem to avoid temptation and desire at this level.

I couldn't find healthy ways to cope. Nothing worked—not the therapy I frequented off and on over the years, not family, not friends. Only a drink brought instant relief. It started slow and steady, then picked up speed. Morning mimosas replaced coffee, wine during the girls' nap times kept me going, and champagne at bedtime felt like my reward for surviving the day. I wanted it. Needed it. So I had it. It all felt justified. What I didn't fully understand at the time was how deeply biology was at play. The brain's reward system, heavily influenced by dopamine, responds strongly to alcohol intake, creating a cycle of craving and temporary satiation. This neurochemical reaction was a physiological hook that made moderation feel nearly impossible, emphasizing that the struggle wasn't simply a moral failure but a strong biological drive.

My drinking escalated, and so did the fights with Peter. I was always defensive, ready to snap. He probably thought I had learned my lesson through the first season of postpartum and wouldn't dare jeopardize our relationship again—who'd be such a fool? Sometimes he deserved my rage, sometimes he didn't, but the truth was it didn't matter—I carried a shield of defensiveness, ready to explode at anything. One drink and I could tip off the edge of reason. Two and a night was shot. I snapped at him over the dishes, laundry, and the worried look he gave me.

I harbored resentment toward him for being at work and not at home, suffering through the day with me. I was mad at our past toxicity and the lack of love and support between us. I often felt that he didn't care about my struggles since he often lacked acknowledgment. The good that I did, all that I could accomplish within a day at home, even though it was minuscule to him, wasn't appreciated in the way I needed it to be. So, I would drink and wait for him to say something stupid enough for me to explode from and then let it all out.

I could feel his disappointment and the growing distance between us. I hated that I was hurting him and hated that he could see it. Our home began to mirror the chaos inside me, and the environment was anything but healthy.

My girls were too young to understand what was happening, but they could feel it too. Piper clung to me when I poured a drink, unaware of the effects it would have on her and Tilly. A wave of guilt washed over me every single time I'd take a sip. I'd pop open a new bottle, wishing the pressure in my chest would release along with the bottle.

I met Peter during my heavy drinking years—he's never really known me sober, so I told myself I'd slow down once we got into a relationship. I wanted to be the woman who sipped wine over dinner with him, not the one who drained bottles behind his back. I tried to match his pace so I wouldn't outdrink him. But old habits don't disappear with a wedding ring—they just change shape. Every glass, I kept telling myself it was just for fun, just to unwind. But when stress piled up, so did the number of drinks. Maybe part of me resisted sobriety because I was scared—terrified, actually—to find out who I was without alcohol. What if I didn't like her?

I liked drinking. I craved it. The taste of a crisp sauvignon blanc, the fizz of champagne on my tongue, the warmth crawling down my throat felt like the only thing that could settle the waves crashing in my head.

So, I ignored what it was taking from me: my marriage, my children's safety, my ambitions, my body. I kept reassuring myself it wasn't that bad. I was still standing, still getting through the days, still doing what needed to be done. I wasn't some woman on a park bench clutching a brown paper bag—I was a mom with a wine glass. Just a "normal" mom, or so I told myself.

Except I wasn't normal. This behavior is not normal.

Peter made comments about how much I was drinking and how I wasn't hiding it as well as I thought, but he hadn't given me a final ultimatum yet, so I kept pushing. I still felt like I had time. I needed to take this as far as I could before I could surrender. Life dragged on, and I could feel myself breaking down from the inside out. I know how dramatic that sounds, but if you've been there, you understand.

I was unraveling, and I could feel it physically. Exhaustion clung to me. My body was shutting down—weight was rapidly declining, hair was thinning, skin was sallow, and eyes were hollow. I was dying from the inside out and still telling myself I was "fine" even though I knew that I was literally killing myself. The decay that's occurring while you're actively living. That slow unraveling brought me closer to my breaking point. There comes a point where you can literally feel yourself ache from the inside out with the knowledge that if something doesn't quickly change, you will most certainly end up in jail or dead.

How bad can bad get? How far gone is too far? I wasn't sure where my rock bottom was or if I really even had one, but I pushed myself to the very edge of finding out. I practiced hitting up different liquor stores, so I wouldn't look like a regular. I made sure I would stock up so I wouldn't run out. Drinking at doctor appointments, therapy sessions, in the shower, in parking lots. I continued making excuses, feeling sorry for myself, and justifying it all. I'd hit my lowest, and it was impossible to deny it any further, no matter how hard I tried.

I kept promising myself I'd cut back—no more drinking in the car (wild, I know), or around the kids. I'd plan to start fresh on Monday. But when those Mondays came, I always found a reason to give in. I convinced myself that if I didn't drink, I'd miss out on something, it wouldn't be as fun, or I couldn't handle daily stress. God forbid I face life challenges clearheaded. I knew I needed to quit, but I just didn't want to—at least not yet. Asking for help meant admitting I'd really messed up, and that's a painful thing to face.

This is what addiction looks like. It doesn't care who you are or where you come from. You probably know someone—a coworker, a friend, a family member—who is struggling, and you may not even realize it. Sometimes it's the "fun" one, the outgoing one, maybe the one who seems to have it all together. Sometimes it's you. The difference between recovery and letting addiction win is being able to admit you have a problem.

I thought I had tried quitting before, but I never actually followed through. Instead, I just made excuses for myself and took more time to try again. *There's always next week,* I would think to myself. *I can start again after the weekend.* If there was even a glimpse of a social event coming up, I *obviously* needed to wait until it was over to stop drinking. How do people do weddings or birthday parties without alcohol? It seemed foreign and straight-up stupid to me.

I honestly had no idea who I was anymore, and sometimes I still don't. When you have been drinking your whole adult life, alcohol colors every decision, every memory. Good or bad, they're all influenced by a buzz.

Peter had both feet out the door, but his heart was still in the house. Chance after chance had been given with no change on my part, but this time, for the first time, I acknowledged that I was sick. I was carrying the burden of alcoholism. My addiction had grown unchecked, leaving it nowhere else to fester. I asked for help, and though his attempts to support me initially stirred anger in me, it was clear that this environment could not continue for the sake of our children. I was the common denominator in the problems we faced, and I needed to take responsibility.

In taking responsibility, though, I realized it wasn't just about holding myself accountable for past mistakes; it was about embracing a path towards healing. For the first time, I began to see that nurturing myself could coexist with accountability. In accepting my own role in the chaos, I also opened the door to self-compassion. This journey was not only about addressing my faults but also about fostering a kinder, gentler relationship with myself that could sustain the changes I needed to make.

I locked myself in the bathroom and cried while lying on the cold tile until I had nothing left. I barely recognized myself when I looked in the mirror. That was the moment my mind finally broke through the denial. *You need help. Now.*

I had nothing left in me. I couldn't hold onto this version of myself anymore. It was breaking my heart, and clearly his, too, so I did the only thing I knew to do in that exact moment—tell him the truth. Not the polished version, but the raw and agonizing truth.

One night, I sat down and wrote him an email. I couldn't say it out loud; the words were too difficult to speak, so I typed them instead. I've never been a good communicator off the cuff. As an empath and highly sensitive individual, I need more time to process my feelings and gather my thoughts, especially when it comes to something so serious. My hands shook as I sat down at the computer and poured my heart out, speaking my truth. The words flowed through me and onto the page as I pleaded my case. I needed him to know that I knew he knew. I needed to tell him that I wasn't strong enough to get a handle on this alone. I wanted him to see my vulnerability and desperation. I admitted what I had been denying: I had a problem. I needed help. And I was scared. Scared of what he would say, but even more scared of what he would do if I didn't get it. I did what I should've done long ago and asked him to step in—to make the decision for me to seek help outside of our home.

Peter, Sunday, October 29, 2023, 5:26pm

I'm so embarrassed and ashamed of having this conversation with you. I know this isn't what you signed up for, or what you would ever want for you or your children. It's not what I want for them either, and I pray they never remember this of me.

Whether you choose to stay in this marriage or not, I have to do this for myself in order to be a better person and mom. I know that I'm at a point where there are no more options.

And if you decide to divorce me, maybe you'll use this against me, but I pray for our girls' sake you don't. A part of me wants to believe that I can do this alone, but I know I need support from people who love me and believe in me. I hope it's you, but I genuinely understand if it's not. I don't want to put this on my mom with everything she's going through with her cancer, and I'm embarrassed for anyone outside of our home to know what a fuck up I've been.

Admitting it was both defeating and relieving. I knew I couldn't climb out alone, and for the first time in a long time, I wanted to try. The trauma I'd carried for years—emotional neglect, old grief, self-sabotage—was finally surfacing.

They say that everyone's rock bottom looks different, and mine wasn't one single incident. No spectacular crashes, cops, or headlines. No DUIs or jail time. No red flags from my doctors about my declining health, even though I was drinking in the car just before checking in for my appointment. Just a thousand small failures piled high, with my conversation with Peter about my email being the top that tipped it all over. Failed promises. Failed mornings. Failed attempts to quit. And the quiet dread of knowing if something didn't change, I would end up dead—and my kids would end up motherless.

My greatest fear was not being with my girls to raise them and watch them grow, yet I consciously chose to jeopardize our future every day. I'm the one who made my fear a real possibility. I teetered so close to the edge so many times that I was fully aware of how close I was to falling at the tail end of my active addiction. The idea of my children having to bury me before they even had a chance to know me broke my heart. This was the very first time I transferred the power to someone else to help me decide how to get better. And while I wasn't absolutely sure of what Peter would do with my written confession, I had a feeling. I had hope.

Let's Reflect

1. What are some healthy coping mechanisms you can implement when you feel triggered?

2. How can you best work through the resentments you hold towards others?

3. What relationships are you afraid will be affected if you don't make positive changes?

4. What emotions are you trying to hide from?

Let's Affirm It

I am worthy of my greatest desires.

Statistically Speaking

30% to 50% of women consume alcohol in the year following birth. (Source: National Library of Medicine 2023)

Part Five: Superhero School

"I thought I would be able to stop on my own, but I couldn't.

I was embarrassed to ask my husband for help and didn't want

to be a disappointment to my family by admitting I needed

to go to treatment. It's so much harder than people think t

o admit you have a problem you can't control."

–Courtney L., mother of three, sober six years

Peter made it very clear that he had done exactly what I had

asked of him; he was getting me help. Days after that email,

he made dozens of phone calls, scrambling to make suitable

arrangements and checking our insurance coverage to ensure

I would receive the best possible care during this transition.

He was giving me the help my life depended on, so yes, I was

going to go somewhere. I, on the other hand, remained in

denial until the evening before I was supposed to check into treatment. I ignored the empty suitcase as long as I could and refused to start packing until I drank as much as I could in those last moments of freedom. I didn't even try to hide it at that point. I just wanted to snuggle on the couch with my babies and have "one more" glass of wine.

I called my mom over to ask if she could help with the girls while I was away at my "wellness retreat." That's literally what I called it, not wanting her to know where I was really going. I couldn't anticipate how she would react if she knew the truth, and I wasn't emotionally equipped to handle any more disappointment or judgment. I framed my leaving as a relaxing and rehabilitating getaway for overworked and tired mothers, a time where I could focus on getting healthy (I had lost a significant amount of weight during active addiction) and get some sleep. She was happy for me and excited for me to hopefully return as a new woman, a new mother. She could see I was hurting and wanted to help me but knew that she couldn't heal me. I gave the nanny the same explanation, and she also offered up any and all free time she had to help take care of the girls. For them, I am forever grateful for their stepping in to nurture and love my girls while I was gone, while I was trying to nurture and love myself.

Peter and I celebrated our wedding anniversary the night before I left for treatment at our favorite celebration restaurant. A place we went for birthdays, anniversaries and big life-changing moments. We ate fantastic food from the chef's tasting menu and drank the finest wines recommended by the sommelier, who knew us well from our frequent visits to the restaurant. How surreal it is to be sitting at a beautiful dinner, drinking with my husband, the knowledge of rehab admission less than 24 hours away playing in my mind. Defiance, denial, and surrender sat at the table with us that night.

I struggled with what to tell Piper and Tilly about where I was going. They were too young to comprehend the truth and wouldn't be able to fully understand what was happening, so I told them the only lie I could think of: Superhero School. A place where I would get healthy, learn some really cool stuff, and gain some power. A place where mommies go to learn how to be super strong and the best moms ever. That part was true. But I was still mad and resentful. I was sad and defeated.

I was embarrassed, and inside, I was breaking. My babies deserved so much more than I was giving them.

A million thoughts ran through my head as I tossed clothes into a suitcase and sipped my final drink. Would my girls forget about me and think the nanny was their new mom while I was gone? Would they miss me at all? Was Peter going to fall in love with the nanny and leave me when I got back home? What will I tell friends and family? How much do they really need to know? I genuinely thought that maybe, just maybe, there was another way out of this as time ticked toward departure.

A hug and kiss goodbye from the girls wasn't sufficient. I needed them more than I could have imagined. As much as I believed they triggered me at times, their company was also my safe space. I desperately wanted to feel their warmth and keep their scent on me the entire drive to the facility. For the first time in their lives, I was leaving them not just for a night, but for a whole month. Was I really going? I continued to quietly weep, earning side glances from my husband as he squeezed my hand. I held harder onto his, pretending to be mad at him for making me go, when in reality, I was mad at myself for what I was doing to my family and my marriage. I can only imagine how he felt driving his wife to rehab— something I can assure you he never envisioned as a part of his happily ever after.

The drive felt like an eternity as the city view slipped away and the rolling hills with barren trees took its place. There was no sun, and the low-lying grey clouds surrounded our car. Despite the gloomy Michigan rain, the air felt cold yet still when I cracked the passenger window in desperation to take a deep breath. We were halfway there when the tears burned my cheeks as I reached for another tissue. My eyes felt heavy, and my heart raced faster with every mile closer. Peter held onto my hand the whole drive, not speaking a word. Not needing to.

About a year before I went into my own treatment, one of my best friends, Tricia, had confided in me that she also had been struggling with alcoholism.

I remember the day she reached out to me, asking to meet for a cup of coffee, and I felt slightly nervous as I hadn't spoken to her in several weeks. I had a feeling that she had something big going on in her personal life, being a mom like me with two small children. She worked full-time as a therapist, was married, and, from the outside, appeared happy. If you had told me she was in rehab for alcohol, I would've laughed in your face and said, "No way. Not her."

When I tell you that I had no idea that one of my best friends of over 15 years—nearly my entire adult life—was an alcoholic, I genuinely had NO idea. Not even the slightest suspicion. I don't remember her ever drinking much in our early twenties. In fact, she was always the responsible one of the bunch, the one mothering us whenever the rest of us were too drunk to find our way home. She was the one making sure we were safe and never seemed to have a hangover the following morning.

However, over the last few months, as we've seen each other at birthday parties and whatnot, I've noticed a gradual shift in my friend's behavior each time I see her. Always frantic and stressed out, she moved through conversations like someone hopped up on who-knows-what. I mentioned it to my mom and a mutual close friend who also noticed this difference within her, but we dropped the topic and moved on. She's never been the type to share her personal struggles with us, so I figured if she wanted to talk about it, she would.

Our kids are very close in age, and we experienced pregnancy together. Attending our children's birthday parties together and complaining to each other about the exhaustion of motherhood was part of the territory. We had survived life's ups and downs together, but alcoholism was a down that she tackled and triumphed in private.

As we sat in the café's corner with our coffees, she shared her struggles and story with me. I was in shock and awe at her secret and at her success. Here was one of my best friends, sharing her journey and experience with treatment and recovery. Openly and vulnerably.

Tears in my eyes, I kept asking, "Why didn't you tell me? Why didn't you let me help?" Which felt like a contradiction since I myself was currently going through the exact same thing. Unable to ask one of my best friends for support or help navigating through my own drinking, I already understood why she never mentioned it. I was drinking twenty-four seven and needed and wanted help, but didn't tell her either. I heard myself in her words. I felt my chest tighten with every mention of hiding bottles and drinking throughout the day. Even though it was her story, it was also my reality.

Now I was the one not sharing my struggle with her. I just let her sobriety success give way to a little bit of hope for myself, and what I knew I inevitably would also experience. I told her how proud I was of her, and I quietly mentioned that I had been drinking a lot lately. I left out the part that I was, without a doubt, an alcoholic and needed to go to treatment too.

She described her experience in treatment as transformative and actually enjoyable. I bookmarked the conversation in my mind, knowing I may revisit the idea of getting treatment there one day myself. If she could get better, why couldn't I? When it came time for me to follow in her footsteps, I shared with Peter the name of the facility and asked him to take the lead on arranging my stay.

Even though I have been on the other side of the coffee table and was now the one in the car on the way, I still didn't want people to know that I was going to treatment. Maybe it was shame and embarrassment, the recognition that I had become a statistic and would be forever known as an addict. The fear of judgment or people coming out of the woodwork, saying, "I knew it." It was yet another secret I chose to keep close to my heart.

What a shame that we were going through the exact same thing at the same time, but didn't know how to share it, to sit in that shared trauma together? We could've supported each other and confided in one another, possibly helped each other avoid the inevitable a little longer. If only we had known. If only we had spoken up. I didn't need to ask her why she never told me; I knew. She felt the shame and embarrassment that comes along with the stigma of being an alcoholic. But here's the thing about stereotypes: they're bullshit. My friend didn't fit the part; she didn't look like an addict. Alcoholics aren't always homeless and unkempt; they're doctors and lawyers, teachers and churchgoers. *Mothers.* Alcoholism knows no limits. It's fair game for any and all of us. Over 28.9 million Americans struggle with drinking, but over 85% receive some type of treatment. I needed to be a part of that statistic.

I came to the realization that rock bottom isn't a place—it's the point where you stop digging. It's the moment you're too tired to keep up the facade. The moment your mind, body, and soul all connect together to say, "This is it. It's time." Only then, when you finally look up and decide to climb, can the next chapter of your life begin.

Pulling up to treatment felt like a prison sentence about to begin. A large, black iron gate opened to allow us through as we circled the cul-de-sac to the main entrance. I stepped out of the car and took a deep breath. The cold air filled my lungs as warm tears filled my eyes and hung from my lashes, momentarily blurring my vision. Broken and empty, I scanned my surroundings in search of something to lock in on— something to make me feel grounded. I spotted a deer peering back at me through the trees. Silent and as still as I was. It was as if it were here to help me find the courage to take my first step through the door. It was as if the deer's eyes were saying: *See? You're not alone.*

I can still feel the pen in my hand hovering above the paperwork. The weight of signing away my freedom, revealing my past, and succumbing to this disease was suddenly a tangible reality. I told myself I wouldn't stay here longer than three days just to make treatment feel less scary, less committed. I don't remember what was discussed at the table as they recited off rules and expectations during my stay. I do recall the intake room feeling much warmer than outside. It only housed a table and a few chairs, but the air was heavy with my anxiety.

My cheeks stained from tears, I hesitantly answered the admission coordinator's questions, my husband bearing witness to what I could no longer keep quiet. A visibly pregnant nurse entered the room and asked me to undergo a breathalyzer—right there in front of my husband and staff. Peter's hand rested on my back, which felt half like a gesture of comfort and half like a nudge off the cliff. All eyes on me, I maintained the story that I hadn't drank that day. I hesitantly took the breathalyzer, the air in my lungs pushing out the breath as almost a sigh of relief, and although the nurse saw that I was lying, she said nothing out loud to call me out in front of the others. She gave me a look that said, "I know, but I won't tell. You're going to be okay." The coordinator continued on about the admittance process while two male techs rummaged through my suitcases. I watched them remove nearly everything I had thoughtfully packed and confiscated everything that could've been used to harm myself, mainly my medications and standard beauty products that contained trace amounts of alcohol.

Once all of the paperwork was completed and signed, Peter and I exchanged goodbye hugs on the front porch. A slight smile spread across his face, letting me know I was making the right decision and that I would be missed at home. He promised to return home and kiss the girls for me and told me not to worry. I watched Peter pull out of the property and through the iron gate. I felt abandoned immediately. I was in the middle of nowhere with a house full of strangers. Addicts. And he just left me here.

I took a few moments to compose myself, wiping the endless tears that were falling and taking yet another deep breath of the still, frigid air. Walking back into the lobby and living space, I observed that the other residents and all of the staff seemed genuinely happy, even laughing, and it annoyed me. How could anyone be happy when they're in rehab? How long had these people freakin' been here? How could you possibly find joy and comfort among these walls?

After the nurse and I completed the rest of the medical intake paperwork, I went straight to my room to cry in private, where I cried for the next seventy-two hours straight. I avoided everyone except the nurse, skipped meals, and left my room only when I truly had to. I sat on the bed, flipping through photo albums of the girls I had made for this "trip", and placed framed photos around the room. No matter which direction I looked, I'd see their sweet faces looking back at me, reminding me why the hell I was even here. To get better. To heal. To relearn how to live.

Let's Reflect

1. What emotions resurfaced when the numbing stopped working?

2. What small, ordinary moments feel terrifying without the crutch—silence, evenings, celebrations, loneliness?

3. What does self-care actually mean for you—beyond bubble baths and buzzwords?

4. How do you forgive the version of you who was just trying to survive?

Let's Affirm It

Healing doesn't feel good at first; it feels heavy.

Statistically Speaking

Within the first three months of sobriety, over 70% of women report heightened anxiety, irritability, and emotional exhaustion—yet also describe deeper clarity and connection by six months. (Source: Journal of Substance Abuse & Recovery, 2023)

Part Six: Rehab Rookie

*"Stop trying to earn rest. You don't have to hit burnout before
you're allowed to take a break. Recovery and motherhood are
both full-contact sports. You can't do either well if you're
constantly abandoning yourself. And finally: you don't have
to do it perfectly. But you do have to do it authentically."*
–Trica Cassady LMSW/CCTP, mother of two, sober 3 years

If you're like I once was, you picture rehab or a treatment
facility to have a specific look and feel to it. I pictured a
shabby shack of a place with hospital floors and dimly lit
hallways. Sterile and stark, beds stripped down to the sheets
with nothing on the walls. I imagined feeling the cold radiate
through the barred windows as gray clouds loomed outside.
The barren trees mark the landscape as desolate. I imagined

addicts rocking in the corner from withdrawals, their hospital gowns barely hanging on their shoulders.

This facility had none of that. This place looked like a large, cozy home, complete with several fireplaces and a small creek running through the property, which sat on several acres. The house was warm, the staff overall quite kind, but I still felt cold, alien, and suffocated.

While the accommodations were nicer than I had expected, rehab didn't feel like salvation **at first**. I felt like I was in a luxury jail with heated bathroom floors and yoga in the mornings. Staff monitoring my movements and interactions, I am now a patient with an assignment and schedule.

The group sessions began with shared laughter and the warmth of collective stories. At first, I stayed distanced, listening from the safety of my room. For the first three days, I refused to join. I holed up in my room, angry and ashamed. I told myself I wasn't like them, that I wasn't 'bad enough.' But then, something began to shift. It was when I overheard someone say, 'You belong here, you're not broken,' that a small crack formed in my wall of self-doubt. Gradually, I joined the group sessions. I listened, hesitated, and then spoke.

Soon, I noticed a flicker of connection I had not felt before. Eventually, I could say, with some disbelief, 'I felt happy.' This would have seemed impossible just days before. Through this juxtaposition, my transformation became clear: from feeling out of place to finding peace.

As much as those first few days wrecked me and as much as I fought it, rehab wasn't this cold and sterile facility. It wasn't padded walls and cafeteria food. It was surreal: yoga mats stacked in the corner of a Planet Fitness-sized gym, an infrared sauna humming beyond the double doors, two chefs who would cook whatever you wanted for every meal, meeting any dietary restrictions or needs. A hair salon and massage table with on-call staff, nature walks scheduled like field trips, as deer galloped across the meadow in the dewy mornings. The creek babbling along the length of the property. On paper, it looked like a wellness retreat, and in some ways, it very much was. That's how I framed it to my mother and nanny when it was time to pack up and go for the month ahead anyway. I was taking some time to work on my health, both physically and mentally. No one needed to know the extent or desperation behind it. No one needed to know where I was really going.

But as nice and accommodating as the facility was, it didn't come close to a relaxing getaway, even with those bonus amenities. All of the above-mentioned fluff was happening behind a locked gate. As much as I was here at will, I wasn't allowed to just walk away. There was a strict and very full schedule to follow every day. I was allowed my phone during set and censored hours each day, as well as minimal access to my laptop, which stayed under lock and key.

The luxury surrounding me didn't soften the truth: this was a bubble where you were stripped down to your ugliest truths. Every day was jam-packed with group sessions, therapy, and "homework." We wrote essays about our triggers, listed gratitude until the word lost meaning, sat in circles where people wept and raged and confessed the wreckage of their lives. It was just as relatable as it was unbearable at times. The connection we all held was undeniable.

As time went on and the days began to weave into each other, something softened. A nurse with kind eyes saw through the walls I'd built, and for the first time in years, I let myself be cared for without earning it. She sat on the edge of my bed flipping through my photo albums, asking me questions about my babies—genuinely curious about who I was and the journey that brought me there. She gently encouraged me to be proud of myself for even walking through the door and nudged me out of my room. I remember her saying, "They're going through the exact same shit you are. I promise it'll get better." And it did.

As I tiptoed towards the fridge for another water (it was slim pickings on the beverage front), one of the other residents said hi. I was slightly taken aback but shyly replied, "Hello." I remember him making small talk and trying to reassure me that everyone there had felt exactly as I did in that moment. It was totally normal to hide away at first, but he also encouraged me to start working my way out of my room. (I'm lucky I didn't need to actually detox and had zero symptoms of withdrawl) It was then that I went back to my room, showered, and joined the rest of the residents for lunch. Every single one of them went around the table and introduced themselves. Sharing something small about themselves with me. Attempting to connect and comfort with their words. My new friend, who helped me venture out of my room, became my puzzle buddy. Every day, we'd meet in one of the living rooms and silently work on a puzzle together. Never needing to say much, we let the silence speak for us as we quietly healed piece by piece.

The women around me in treatment, once strangers, became mirrors reflecting back my own pain and possibilities. We laughed in the kitchen over burnt toast, we cried in group therapy, we cheered when one of us made it through a day without wanting to run. They reminded me that what I was doing for myself and my children was remarkable, and I was "lucky" to be getting ahead of this disease while they're still so young. That they'll never remember any of this.

I immediately felt a weight lift and an opportunity to breathe again present itself. These people weren't crazy at all; they were exactly like me and here for the same damn reasons. While our stories and journeys that brought us here were different, our desire was the same. To change our lives for the better and give ourselves the chance to start over. I learned that many of the residents had several attempts at recovery with failed success, bringing them back again for another round of hope to fly free from this disease. Through the days and the weeks that passed, I laughed with them, cried with them, and began to feel like maybe I could actually come out on the other side of this. I made friends. We attended meetings together, watched movies together, did puzzles until midnight, and wrote poetry at sunset. We arose with gratitude and recentered ourselves as many times as we needed to throughout the day. We danced to music we wouldn't normally listen to, we set the dinner table like a family, and finished each other's crossword puzzles.

The days were kept full and focused with several educational and psychological group meetings, one-on-one therapy sessions, nature walks, and necessary free time to use the gym and sauna. It sounds super fancy and glamorous, and while all of those things were absolutely luxuries most people don't have access to in these situations, it doesn't feel like a luxury when you're in the middle of reconfiguring your life; it feels more like survival necessities.

All of this cracked something open. I felt the weight on my shoulders start to dissipate. I suddenly felt capable of speaking, of living again, not as who I once was but as my true self.

I showered. I went to lunch. I sat at the table. And for the first time in a long time, I felt happy.

These were no longer strangers. They weren't caricatures

of addicts. They were me. Broken, messy, scared—but still trying. And above it all, they were kind and gentle people. All hurting and healing right alongside me. That resident who first welcomed me, my puzzle partner, the quiet girl I sat next to while eating lunch, they became the keepers of my deepest and darkest secrets. They became my support team.

In their stories, I saw my own. In their pain, I saw my traumas. Family visits came after my first week there, and as I watched my girls walk toward me from the car with Peter, my eyes burned with tears again. Not only was my heart happy to see them, but it was also still embarrassed and ashamed that it was here of all places. I was broken into a million different pieces, still trying to put myself back together. My new friends at the house reassured me that my children were so young that they would never remember this, never know this version of me. Thank God, I told myself, while also secretly sad that they won't witness the intense fight within me to change my life – to change their world. Someday, I'd tell myself – they'll know how hard I fought to be the best version of myself for them. They'll know not just what I've done to get me here, but what it took to get me out.

There was real work to be done. Not just within us, but we had essays to write, homework to complete, and activities that we were required to participate in throughout our stay. Every day began and ended with listing 3 things we were grateful for and a motivational scripture. While all of this was absolutely helpful in early recovery, it's extremely unrealistic. This isn't what life looks like, this bubble of safety and structure. Mornings at home don't look like lists of gratitude and moments of meditative silence, let's be real. As much as I tried to tell myself that things would be different when I got home, that I would be able to handle my shit, I knew deep down that my bubble would burst nearly immediately after walking back through my front door.

During our family visits, we laughed and played, had snacks, and said our goodbyes. We spent Thanksgiving there together, something that was both wonderful and strange. Tears would stream down my face as that damn gate opened and they drove back home – without me. It was heartbreaking each and every time. My babies. My whole world. I was doing this for them, I'd remind myself. I then dedicated every single second of my treatment to surviving this for them. Not only did I stay that first week, but I also survived the second, then the third, and I made it to the very end. I stayed as long as my insurance would pay for – 25 days, and I honestly would've stayed a few days longer if I could've. The cards of life had been laid out on the table, and I had barely begun examining each one when it was already time to leave. I knew that this new lifestyle I had adapted to wasn't sustainable, but I felt confident I would be leaving there with the appropriate tools and attitude to maintain sobriety.

The day had come, and I had finally done it. I had completed everything I was required to, every assignment, every group meeting, every therapy session, every morning check-in. I participated way more than I ever thought I would. I became a voice of reason, support, and motivation for the new residents who had trickled in since I arrived. And at the end of those 25 days, I sat in a circle with my new sober friends, therapists, and husband as each person took turns speaking about me and to me, how proud they were and how sure they were of my success outside of here. How their experience with me had helped **them** heal, when really they all helped me just as much, if not more. After the well wishes were shared and my husband talked about how much he looked forward to this new life together, we stepped outside, and I rang the sacred sobriety bell that's reserved to be rung for only those who complete treatment. The sound echoed between the trees and filled my soul with hope. I did it.

Time served.

Treatment provides a stable, structured environment where the only person you need to take care of is yourself. It provided me with a safe space to share the deepest, darkest parts of myself with people who could understand and relate to them. It allowed me to rest both mentally and physically, with the sleep I had so desperately needed but wasn't getting at home. It provided me with an outlet to move my body and try meditation through yoga. It gave me a place to sweat out toxins in the red-light sauna. It circled me with a community of health providers and caregivers who made me feel like I was more than just a patient. For the first time in a long time, it was the only place I could truly be myself. I grew to enjoy the silence throughout the day during our downtime. Since we weren't allowed to use laptops or cell phones, I went for walks and did word searches. I made jewelry and did puzzles. I wrote poems and did crafts. It slowly started to feel like home, only to be suddenly time to go home.

Rehab is a bubble, yes—but it's also a mirror. It reflects back to you the pieces you've been hiding, the ones you'd rather never look at again. It forces you to sit with them, turn them over in your hands, and decide whether you're going to keep carrying them or finally set them down.

And for the first time, I thought maybe—just maybe—I could survive if I set them down.

I knew I needed that help, but I pushed the idea out of my mind time and time again until I was out of time. I genuinely liked drinking and didn't know how to exist without it until rehab. I craved the taste of a good bottle of Sauvignon Blanc and the fizz of champagne, which slowly turned into a craving for Tootsie Pops and sparkling water instead. I enjoyed the warmth that rushed over me and the calmness it brought to my mind and now craved a good workout and a cup of tea. I felt like it was the only thing that could settle the waves that were constantly crashing in my mind, unaware of my own strength that hid between each white cap. I turned my head to negative effects as much as I could, convinced

I didn't deserve happiness. It was the catalyst for disastrous relationships, was contributing to my marriage falling apart, and it was putting my children's lives and innocent people's lives in danger daily. It stole my time from the things I really wanted to do and replaced it with the idea that I just didn't have the time. It allowed me to make excuses for myself by putting a mask on my actions. In the end, I was just spending all of my time drinking or thinking about when I could savor that next sip. Until I completed treatment, I was brainwashed by the damn stuff.

Let's Reflect

1. What parts of you are you most afraid of rediscovering?

2. Who is most supportive of your journey, and why is it important to you?

3. What masks do you put on in your most vulnerable moments?

4. Do you believe you're worthy of a better life?

5. In what ways do you cope with daily life stressors?

Let's Affirm It

There's always another way, not another day.

Statistically Speaking

1 in 6 deaths among women aged 20–49 are attributable to excessive alcohol use. (Source: National Institute on Alcohol Abuse, 2025)

Part Seven: Pop Goes the Bubble

"Rehab saved my life. It saved my marriage and my family. I never would've been able to crawl out of that hole on my own. I can only pray that I'm strong enough to hold onto what I now have."
–Robyn M., mother of two, sober 18 months

Rehab is a bubble: a weird little world where everyone is rooting for you, restaurant-quality food that you didn't cook appears on plates, and you get praised just for showing up.

It's a strange and temporary world where you start to believe the impossible is possible. But the real world doesn't change while you're busy working on yourself. The people at home remember. The bills wait. The triggers line up, ready to pounce. Leaving treatment wasn't an ending—it was the start of the hardest chapter yet.

Bubbles always burst—and mine did the second I walked back through my front door.

Everything at home was the same—the kids were screaming, the dog was barking, dishes piled up, bills lay on the counter, my husband's wary eyes lay upon me—but I was different. It almost felt like I was set up to fail as much as to succeed. How does one transition from a peaceful, healing environment back into a wild and demanding one? This time around, I didn't have a glass of wine to blur the edges. Everything felt more real and raw now, and I felt overwhelmed almost immediately upon returning home.

The house looked the same, but I didn't. I looked and felt refreshed, my mind clear and focused now, while my home environment reminded me that I didn't have as much control as I thought I did.

I tried to carry rehab's lessons into my living room—gratitude lists, deep breathing, yoga poses before someone spilled milk, and box breathing after. It wasn't glamorous, but it was something.

But then came the fights with Peter. Rehab didn't erase resentment, financial stress, or endless childcare. Sobriety made me more present, but sometimes that just meant being painfully aware of everything broken. It made the pieces that had fallen apart feel that much more jagged and sharp. Words cut deeper now that I could feel them.

And here's the truth no one wants to say out loud: sometimes, sobriety makes everything feel worse before it feels better. Because you're no longer numbing. You're feeling it. All of it.

The routines I built in rehab—gratitude lists, structured days, therapy on tap—evaporated within days of being home. That safe space I had grown accustomed to was no longer. Instead, there were tantrums, sleepless nights, and a husband who didn't exactly greet me with confetti and open arms. He wanted to trust me, but trust isn't rebuilt in twenty-five days.

And the cravings and urges? They didn't stay at rehab either. In treatment, alcohol didn't exist and wasn't even an option. Back home, it was everywhere. On billboards. In commercials. At the grocery store, in restaurants. The siren song of Sauvignon Blanc didn't get quieter just because I'd spent a month in a bubble—it got louder. The realization that I couldn't have it anymore kept running through my head all day long. Instead of thinking about when I'd be able to have my next drink, I spent all of my time thinking about how I couldn't have a drink.

Here's the thing no one tells you about relapse: it isn't just possible, it's probable. According to the National Institute on Drug Abuse, **40– 60% of people relapse within their first year of recovery.** That's not failure. That's the disease. That's reality.

The brain doesn't care that you sat in group therapy or cried in front of a bunch of strangers. It cares that you fed it alcohol for years and then suddenly stopped. It will beg, bargain, scream for relief. And if you're not ready, if you don't have tools stacked like armor back at home, you'll cave.

I knew the odds were against me. And still, I thought I could white-knuckle it at home. I thought I was ready.

Leaving treatment wasn't an ending—it was a beginning. And beginnings are hard.

The routines I built in rehab—lists and mantras, sturdy, structured days, on-call doctor appointments—evaporated as soon as I got home. Suddenly, it was tantrums, sleepless nights, and a husband who didn't yet trust me. Trust takes time, and we weren't there.

I had to learn how to stay when the temptation to run was constant. To pour a drink, to quit, to hide again. I told myself, *Just one. Just today. No one will know. I can start again tomorrow. I doubt I'd even like it anymore.*

But then I'd remember the faces from rehab. The laughter in the kitchen. The strangers who had held up mirrors I didn't want to look into. And I'd remember what they told me: *Don't quit before the miracle. You just have to wait long enough.*

So, I stayed. Messy, angry, exhausted—but sober. I stayed waiting for this miracle people kept mentioning, even when I couldn't feel it, couldn't see it.

Sobriety in the real world isn't an even playing field—it's a battlefield. Every day, I had to choose: pick up a drink or pick myself up. Keep the pieces of my puzzle together or remove one and start again?

Early sobriety is a very specific kind of hell. One that no amount of rehab or therapy can prepare you for. It is where you will be tested as you've never been tested before. Where you'll first-hand see how strong you really are, how strong you have to be. That bubble you were living in while in active addiction has now burst, and you now live in the remnants of it.

Early sobriety is waking up with no hangover yet feeling like you've been hit by a truck. It's the sensation of sandpaper against raw skin, highlighting how every nerve is exposed to a world suddenly too bright and too loud. It's living with your skin turned inside out, where even the faintest touch can be unbearable. Every sound seems amplified, like the clanging of pots in an empty kitchen, and every feeling too sharp to handle. There is nothing that could've prepared me for that kind of twist.

And when you add toddlers to the mix? Forget it. I immediately felt the overwhelm and triggers kick in when I walked back into my home that very first day out of rehab. My girls were excited to see me, of course. They were loud and typical toddlers, but to me, it felt like too much already. I was instantaneously overstimulated and overwhelmed. As a newly sober parent, you get a front row seat to every tantrum, every Cheerio spilled on the floor, every scream about the wrong color sippy cup. There were days in the beginning when I sat on the kitchen tile whispering, *"You're okay, you can do this, you're okay"* like a mantra to myself, just to make it to bath time. There were a lot of tears during those early months when

I thought I was supposed to be overjoyed. Relieved to have gotten a new lease on life. Thankful to be able to feel things like I couldn't before. I remember reading Facebook post after Facebook post about women in early sobriety feeling fantastic. They were healthy and thriving after just 30 days, working out daily and practicing affirmations. They claimed that they had never felt better.

Me? Yeah, no. I didn't relate. I felt like shit still and again felt like I was failing because instead of this sobriety glow up they were having, I was still messy. Why wasn't anyone posting about that? The depression and confusion about who I was felt like betrayal.

Sobriety didn't make me a perfect mom; it made me a real one, though. It made me an available one. Available to talk, listen, and be present. Sometimes, real looks like crying in the shower so your kids don't see, then dancing in the living room to "Wheels on the Bus" five minutes later because they deserve joy, even if you're still barely hanging on. It was hiding in the bedroom for a few minutes for a quick breakdown, only to return to the playdough with staggered breathing and fists clenched with anxiety. I did anything and everything I could to hide how hard this was because relapsing, showing any weakness, would be another failure for not only myself, but for them too.

What I didn't realize in that moment was that I wasn't alone—not by a long shot.

A 2020 RAND Corporation study found that women's heavy drinking days (four or more drinks within a couple of hours) increased by 41% during the pandemic. Among mothers of young children, binge drinking nearly doubled compared to pre-pandemic levels. Women in their 30s and 40s—the exact demographic raising toddlers—are the fastest-growing group of alcohol dependent individuals in the U.S. And here's the kicker: fewer than 1 in 10 women with alcohol use disorder receive any form of treatment.

So, when I thought I was the only mom hiding bottles in laundry baskets or sipping "coffee" that wasn't coffee at 9 a.m., the truth was there were tens of thousands of us—drowning silently in plain sight.

And yet, early sobriety feels like solitary confinement. You're the only one wide awake, seeing every crack in the walls you built. You're the only one shaking through cravings while your kids scream in the background. You're the only one fighting the voice that says, *Just one. Just today. No one will know.*

It's those moments when it feels impossible to step out of the darkness and use your voice. To say, hey, I still need some help here. Or to someone else struggling, let them know that they're not alone and you're happy to sit in that struggle with them.

People like to romanticize recovery: the phoenix rising from the ashes, the glow of a new life. In just a short time, their lives have radically changed, and they're now living their dreams, so you should be too. Let me tell you the truth: it's ugly before it's beautiful. Like really fucking ugly.

Early sobriety was brain fog thick enough to choke on. I was forgetting how to have fun without a glass in my hand. What was I even supposed to be doing with my hands? They were like two foreign objects attached to my body. It was looking in the mirror and wondering, *Who the hell am I without alcohol? Am I still hiding? Am I still a fraud?* For those first few months in recovery, I was convinced I was incapable of staying sober. There was no way I could attend a wedding, throw a party, or enjoy my favorite TV show on the couch without a glass of wine. It wasn't going to be possible to finish my DIY projects without a crisp, cold drink in hand. If I had never done those things before, like ever in my adult life, how the hell was I supposed to do it now?

When you strip away the drink, you strip away the mask. Suddenly, every insecurity you've ever drowned comes roaring back, and we as addicts have no idea what to do with that feeling. We feel naked and exposed to the elements of judgment from others, but even more so, ourselves. Every trauma you've numbed demands to be felt. My therapist told me, *"You have to sit in it now."* I wanted to punch him in the face. My mind replied, *"You sit with it, sir. I'm about tapped out."*

And the cravings? They don't just vanish. Studies show it can take up to two years for the brain's reward system to rewire after heavy alcohol use. Two years of neurons misfiring, begging for the shortcut of a drink. Taunting and teasing you when things start to go awry. Two years of retraining your body to believe that joy, relief, and peace can exist without ethanol in your bloodstream.

That's why relapses are common in the first year—because the body remembers before the mind does.

It was on day 31 that I relapsed. To be honest, it all started with a feeling of restlessness that morning, a nagging voice whispering that maybe I was 'better' now, maybe I had proven my point during rehab, maybe I had a handle on this. This tiny thought sparked the illusion that perhaps I could control it this time. I convinced myself that trying moderation wouldn't hurt, picturing other functional people having a glass or two and managing just fine. I remember heading out that day, driven not by a need to cope but by a dangerous curiosity and misplaced confidence. I can't recall the drive to the store or selecting the bottle, but I vividly remember the sensation of the burn down my throat and the sense of reunion, almost like meeting an old friend. I missed that relaxed warmth enveloping me, and I realized then that it was the comfort I had been longing for.

Looking back, I've recognized that allowing complacency to set in was a critical mistake. Now, I keep a detailed list of my triggers and any potential stressors in a journal to bring awareness to these risks before they become overwhelming. Whenever the urge resurfaces, I reach out to a trusted friend or support group to vocalize my struggles. This open line of communication acts as a safeguard, granting accountability and understanding that I'm not fighting this battle alone.

What I thought was going to be a one-off slip-up became a full-blown relapse immediately. Once you reintroduce alcohol back into your life, it's inevitable that you then hand over control. My mentality was this: *I've already fucked up and had a drink, I might as well keep going. I'll never win.* Why not just keep down the road to relapse instead of turning back to the road of recovery? Drinking again just felt easier to me, and I again started making excuses for myself. So, I kept it up for a solid 10 days straight. Drinking 24/7 and hiding the bottles, thinking I had myself and my husband fooled.

The joke was on me.

I walked through the front door with our oldest daughter one day, and there he was, standing at the kitchen counter. As the rain dripped down my face like freshly fallen tears, my heart jumped as I saw the bottles. Strewn across the counter was the evidence. Over 20 empty bottles sat, pulled from their hiding places, from the bottom of the trash can, and from my car. The disappointment in his eyes kept me locked in position, unable to take a step forward or speak.

When I was finally able to find words, all I could say was, "Where did you get those?" As if they weren't mine and I wasn't a liar. As if he were the one who had done something wrong. This felt worse than before I had gone to treatment when I had asked for help, because at least then I hadn't made the promise to quit and stick with it. It was in that moment that I could see how much I had hurt him, destroying any chance of trust between us. I have to admit that moment nearly ended my marriage, and we are still rebuilding from it to this day.

I promised yet again to get my shit together, unable to offer him a reason or explanation for the slip. Trying to justify it and make excuses for myself, I, too, had trouble trusting myself. The mental sabotage of relapse is just as brutal, if not more so, than the physical. It's not that I didn't learn it in rehab or know the severity of a relapse before it happened, but it was then that I was finally fully ready to commit to sobriety. It took that relapse, that look on his face, and the sound of my children laughing in the living room to really get it into my brain.

You tried to moderate, and you couldn't handle it. You are an alcoholic and always will be.

Now I was ready. Now I deeply longed for it and needed it. This time, I truly wanted it. So, I tried again.

For me, maintaining sobriety wasn't about grand gestures; it was about those small victories that seemed insignificant to others but monumental to me. Imagine setting a two-minute timer on your phone each time an urge hit. Commit to staying sober for just these 120 seconds. Once that timer dings, acknowledge the success and set it for another two minutes if needed. It is in these second-by-second triumphs that a day of sobriety is built.

I didn't restart my sobriety clock (I have no doubt that it makes some people furious), but I personally didn't feel like I should have to. I was sober all through treatment and the first 30 days back home. I'm not dismissing all of that time because of 10 days of stupidity. I kept going because I didn't know what else to do. Something about that second go at it felt a little easier, though, when I was home and in my own environment. I was more comfortable talking about my triggers and asking for help. I didn't feel so much like a failure; I felt like a human who made mistakes and picked themselves back up.

I didn't stay sober in those early months after relapse because I suddenly "loved myself" or "chose better." I stayed sober because I broke it down into the tiniest victories possible.

I wasn't doing the whole "one day at a time." For me, it looked like a second-by-second, minute-by-minute approach.

Survive this morning without drinking.

Survive this afternoon without drinking.

Survive bedtime without drinking.

Then do it again tomorrow. In early recovery, your sobriety is all mental and basically nothing physical anymore. Your brain is still wired to be an addict, and it takes years for that damage to repair itself.

And when the cravings howled loudest, I found new ways to cope. Sometimes it was crouched in the tub, under a too-hot shower, until the water ran cold, while my tears and cravings washed away. Sometimes it was eating my kid's leftover dinosaur nuggets on the kitchen floor because chewing felt safer than pouring. I replaced an alcoholic drink with a non-alcoholic one – and still do daily. Sometimes it was scrolling recovery pages instead of my usual social media, reminding myself I wasn't the only one losing my mind without my crutch. I tried to squeeze in some daytime meetings, but to be honest, that was a struggle for me. I still couldn't connect with a lot of them—Not Wi-Fi connect, but with my head and heart. When they'd ask during the meeting, "How are you doing it, staying sober?" I never gave credit to anyone but myself because I felt like I was the only one who deserved it. I'm the one doing it, I'm putting in the work. No one else in the world can keep me sober except myself, just like no one can maintain your sobriety for you.

These weren't glamorous wins. They weren't Instagram-worthy. But they stacked up slowly until days became weeks, and weeks became months, and months became years. I'd say to someone else struggling now that it's not one day at a time. Just tell yourself you're not going to drink right this minute. Then not this half hour, not this hour, and not this night. Do that over and over until you've gotten through one day, then rinse and repeat. Watch the clock if you need to, tick from minute to minute, with each movement another victory for not drinking.

The truth is, the hard stuff didn't go away when I stopped drinking. But neither did I. Just the opposite happened, actually.

And that—more than anything—is what saved me. I kept

showing up for myself and my girls because the longer I'm sober, the more I realize just how amazing I really am. Just how capable and resilient I am. So are you.

Sobriety didn't fix my marriage; hell, it didn't even help much at all like I had hoped. It didn't erase my depression; it just displaced it somewhere else. It didn't make my kids less needy or my life less chaotic. But it gave me the one thing I had been losing by the glass: clarity.

And slowly, painfully, and awkwardly, I started to believe that who I truly am never had the opportunity to experience life. I had never even given myself a chance to feel things in real time, to make decisions without filling up the tank first, to speak and act with reason.

This is the part no one glamorizes—the shaking, the stillness, the becoming. But it's also where life begins to hum again. Next, we'll step into what it means to rebuild—not just sober, but awake.

Let's Reflect

1. How realistic are the expectations you've set for yourself?

2. Can you confidently enforce boundaries, and if so, what are they?

3. Identify who you look for validation from- is it a healthy relationship?

4. Do your core values align with the relationships you foster?

Let's Affirm It

Your faults and fumbles don't define who you are.

Statistically Speaking

Children of parents in recovery are five times more likely to seek emotional support and mental health care when struggling, compared to children of parents who remain untreated. (Source: National Center on Addiction and Substance Abuse, 2023)

Part Eight: Relearning How to Live

*"I had no idea I had a target on my back as a woman and a mother.
The glamorized glass of wine at the pool or the beach quickly turned into
overindulging, failed moderation, hangovers, anxiety, shame, and—most
importantly—missing out on the beautiful moments I should've been
fully present with my kids. I wish I'd known sooner how much
alcohol was taking from my life, instead of adding to it. I wish I'd
known it's possible to live a full, happy life without it."*
–Heather S., mother of three, sober two and a half years

I used to think self-care was bullshit. A marketing scam for
bath bombs and overpriced face masks that never really do
anything. Who had time for that when there were diapers to
change, snacks to sweep up and serve out, and tiny dictators
to keep alive? I've never been someone who frequented nail

or hair salons, got massages, or facials. I wouldn't have defined self-care as anything but that. Do you?

Sobriety forced me to rethink that. Because the truth is, self-care isn't selfish at all. It's a large part of sobriety survival, and it can come in many different forms. It may not look the same to me as it does to you, and vice versa, which is how it should be. We're not cookie-cutter molds, so why should our self-care and recovery be?

In early recovery, my showers became my sanctuary as I mentioned before. I'd stand under the water until it ran cold, sometimes three times a day, just to feel the weight lift for a moment. It was the only place I could breathe without judgment, where no one needed me, where I could cry without scaring my kids, and just be alone. Where I felt like the urges, cravings, and feelings of distress wash away. My kids might stand outside the bathroom door, hysterical, begging to come in, but at least in the shower, I could be alone. I started this therapeutic practice early on in treatment, the shower being the only place on the property I felt I could release everything. I can proudly say I was the cleanest resident there.

But self-care wasn't just showers. I was letting myself cry

in the car after preschool drop-off instead of swallowing it down. Shedding those tears without even knowing where they were coming from or stemmed from. It was sitting on the floor, coloring next to my daughters with the expensive markers and an adult coloring book I bought just for me. It was five barefoot minutes outside, toes in the grass, whispering to the sky, *"Please surround me with peace and patience. Ground me."*

I had to unlearn the toxic mantra I'd lived by: that rest is a reward. Sobriety taught me that rest is part of the work. Rest is where repair happens, and it's a necessary part of healing. And when I finally allowed myself to stop hustling for worthiness, to stop trying to earn every breath of relief, something shifted. I started prioritizing myself, even if that meant taking just a few minutes out of the day or an hour after the kids went to bed to do whatever the hell I wanted. Put my laundry away and paint my toenails or do a face mask while watching a show that I wanted to watch. Watering the flowers, taking the time to write, learning how to meditate (honestly, I still suck at it), that's all self-care.

Relearning life sober is awkward as hell.

It's going to a birthday party and realizing you have no

idea what to do with your hands without a drink or clutching a bottle of water so tightly your knuckles turn white. Constantly sipping on something in order to avoid the temptation.

It's sitting at dinner with friends and feeling like the only alien in the room when the waiter asks, *"Can I get you a drink?"* It's sex without liquid courage, confronting every insecurity head-on, and being aware of your body. It's conversations where you actually remember what you said the next morning and don't owe apologies. It's being weirdly self-aware.

And in that awkwardness, there's growth. Because you don't have the escape hatch anymore. You're forced to be fully present, even when it's uncomfortable, even when it sucks, and you allow yourself for the first time ever to be authentically you.

This isn't just touchy-feely. The science backs it up. Researchers call it *neuroplasticity*—the brain's ability to rewire itself. When you've been drinking heavily, your brain literally reshapes around alcohol, creating neural highways that scream for the substance. It's like when people ask you why can't you just stop drinking? Because it's a disease that you mentally have relinquished all control to. Take alcohol away, and those pathways don't just vanish. They have to be rewired, rebuilt, and replaced with new habits. That doesn't happen overnight.

That's why recovery isn't just about not drinking. It's about retraining your entire body and mind to live and think. Pause here for a moment – how many people do you know who have had to reteach themselves how to live as a part of society? Have you had to completely hit the reset button and start all over? Recovery is and will continue to be something so sacred that not everyone can successfully go through it. So, bravo to you if this is the path you choose.

Cravings don't magically disappear; they're rerouted. Coping mechanisms don't materialize; they're built, brick by brick, day by day.

And yes, it's exhausting. It takes time—studies suggest up to **two years** for the brain's stress-response systems to stabilize after quitting alcohol. Two years of practice, patience, and repetition. Two years of creating new rituals that don't end with a cork pop.

When people hear "self-care," they imagine spa days, yoga retreats, bubble baths, and candles on Instagram. But sobriety self-care is basic, almost embarrassingly small. It's drinking water before coffee, reminding yourself to breathe, and feeling the ground beneath your feet. It's eating breakfast and going to bed before midnight. It's texting someone instead of spiraling alone, and saying no when you want to say yes just to please someone else. Water, Breathe, Ground. It's not glamorous or Instagrammable, but it rebuilds trust in yourself, which is worth more than any filter.

The hardest part wasn't the cravings—it was the silence.

For years, I drowned out my thoughts with alcohol. Without it, the quiet was deafening. My therapist told me I had to "feel my feelings." I wanted to punch him, but he was right. Sobriety forced me to sit in sadness and let grief and anger wash over me, instead of running.

Some days, that meant lying in bed, letting myself cry it out. Other days, it was staring at the wall in chaos, reminding myself, *You don't have to fix everything right now. Just survive this moment.* And little by little, I did.

Here's the thing: it doesn't stay all raw and ugly forever. I promise, it doesn't.

Over time, the awkwardness softened. The silence became bearable. Then, surprisingly beautiful. I noticed things again—

the sound of my daughters' laughter, the way the air smelled after rain, the way my body felt after a good night's sleep. I started to feel alive, in a way I hadn't in years.

Sobriety didn't make life easier. It made it clearer. Better.

And when I look back now, I realize: self-care wasn't about bubble baths or green smoothies. It was about rebuilding myself from the ground up. Teaching myself how to rest. Teaching myself how to cope. Teaching myself how to live without a crutch. Teaching myself that I am, in fact, worthy.

That's the real work. The messy, unglamorous, beautiful work.

Another part of self-care is allowing the bad days to come too. No one is happy all the time, and the lows are just as important as the highs. The difference between sadness in active addiction and recovery is that when sober, you can ask yourself why. Why do you feel sad, and what is the root of it? Process it, feel it, and let it do its thing. I promise it'll make you stronger than if you try to fight it.

The point is, if you feel sad or depressed, try to embrace it rather than reason with it. Move through it slowly and allow those feelings to do what they need to do. Don't fight the tears, don't get upset with yourself, and don't believe for a single second that there's something wrong with you. Remember—this is a completely different version of you. I had to relearn how to feel and how to function without the crutch of alcohol. I was forced to sit with my thoughts and the consequences of those without being able to blame anything on being under the influence. Too many times to count, I would have to remind my husband early on that this is the first time in my adult life that I'm 100% sober and having to deal with life on life's terms. I had to figure out how to alter my reactions and actions according to the situation at hand entirely on my own. As terrifying as that is, it's also an insanely beautiful experience and not something everyone can do successfully.

While I consider myself a writer, I'm still not a journaling person. Mantras and affirmations don't always land for me. But when I can pause, even for a moment, and say, "I'm okay right now," that's become enough. And sometimes, enough is everything. We, as addicts in recovery, need to alter (not lower) our expectations of ourselves and often those we love the most to fit the moment. We will falter and fail, but so will they in their support for us. I wanted people to constantly check in on me and praise me for still being sober. I wanted my sobriety to be as important to them as it was and is to me, but that's never the case. Take ownership of your experience, every single second of it. Develop an understanding that support will come in different ways from different people, and that expecting their journey beside you to be parallel is unreasonable.

My husband isn't a very excitable person to begin with, but I anticipated this world of constant praise and acknowledgment from him that never really came. That bothered me, but it shouldn't because he shows support in other ways. Try to be open to the possibility that people will be there for you in ways you didn't originally anticipate. If I told him I wanted to go to a meeting, he'd say, go. If I said I was feeling triggered, he'd ask why. Those small, simple interactions are a form of support and his way of showing me he cares that I want to stay sober.

The world won't hand you permission to care for yourself—you'll have to take it back. The next chapter explores what happens when self-care becomes self-trust, and you start building a life that actually fits.

Let's Reflect

1. What does self-care look like when no one is watching?

2. Which parts of your routine are about numbing, and which are about nourishing?

3. What boundaries would you set if guilt weren't part of the equation?

4. How does your body tell you it's depleted, and how often do you listen?

5. When did "rest" start to feel like weakness, and what would it take to reclaim it as power?

Let's Affirm It

Rest is not laziness. It's a rebellion against a world that profits from your exhaustion.

Statistically Speaking

Mothers, on average, spend 97% of their waking hours doing something for someone else. Only 26% report dedicating even 15 minutes daily to intentional self-care. (Source: Pew Research Center, 2024)

Part Nine: Generational Curse

"My entire family drinks, so I never thought I really had a problem. It wasn't until my dad died of cirrhosis that I saw how far gone I was too. It really woke me up and made me change the trajectory of my own life."

–Samantha Rossi, mother of four, sober eight years

My father was an alcoholic.

That sentence used to feel like an accusation or a prison sentence; now it feels like an explanation. Now, as an adult, as an addict….I understand him more than I ever have.

When I was a kid, I didn't call it addiction. I just called it normal because that's the only version of him that I knew. I heard my parents fighting behind closed doors, whether they attempted to hide it or not; the sharp crack of his belt when we had done something wrong; the tension that hung heavy in the house, like the smoke from his cigarettes. I didn't know he'd been to treatment until I went myself; my mom never told me, although I wish she had. Maybe he and I would've been able to talk about that and finally form a relationship as adults.

She struggled to keep her feelings about him separate from how she raised us, and the occasional silence spoke louder than words ever could. He was a failure and disappointment to her, making him a failure and disappointment to us, too. I didn't know the struggles that he faced or how hard he fought to get better time and time again. The lack of support he had and the judgment from my family he had endured. I ask myself whether it would've made a difference in our relationship or changed the way I looked at him, and the answer is – yes. A big resounding yes.

Back in my early teens and into adulthood, I told myself I'd never end up like him. That I'd be different. And yet, decades later, I was hiding bottles in closets and lying to the people who loved me most, just like he did. Everything I claimed to never emulate became my new identity.

Addiction is generational. Studies show that children of alcoholics are **four times more likely** to develop alcoholism themselves. Which is terrifying as a parent. It doesn't matter how many times you swear you'll never touch a drop—the pattern is there, waiting, whispering and welcoming you. I thought I was immune. I wasn't.

But here's the thing about cycles: they can be broken. You can be the one to break them.

I looked at my girls through my active addiction, knowing that I was walking the road that my dad walked. As desperate and determined as I was to avoid it, I dragged my feet toward an inevitable ending. I didn't want to put the burden of my addiction on my children.

I no longer have to lie in bed at night full of regrets or anxiety from my actions. I lifted and discarded the weight of the curse and put it so far aside from my life that it can never touch them. I own and possess the power to change their future by changing my own.

I've been working through my traumas with my therapist, and honestly, I didn't even realize they were traumas at first. I never saw having an abusive, alcoholic father as "traumatic." Or being sexually abused by a family member—because in my mind, it didn't seem "bad enough." If something didn't kill me, how could it be trauma? If other people had it worse off, then why should I play a victim? I now understand trauma and PTSD can look very different for everyone. You don't have to almost die for something to cut you deeply and leave a scar—and you don't have to let it define you, either.

My father often let me down, broke promises, and left us begging him for food and money. That fear of being abandoned shaped my relationships—always making me wonder if I was good enough. I'd settle, just to avoid being alone, putting myself in uncomfortable or even unsafe situations because I wanted to be chosen, to feel wanted. That often meant joining in with whatever the crowd was doing—drinking, drugs, anything to belong. It was easier to go along than to stand out, even if it meant following people down bad paths. I still feel that old pressure to fit in, to be needed. I was never the popular girl in school, and I never really knew why I didn't have many friends. What was wrong with me? Or maybe the better question is, what was wrong with my perspective of the people I was so desperate to fit in with?

I've always needed to belong, and I still question my motives—am I doing this for me, or to look better or more likable to others? I care way too much about what people think. I'm an empath, always tuned in to others' feelings, sometimes to my own detriment. Alcohol and drugs gave me a mask—I could be whoever I thought people wanted. The fun one, the party girl. But no matter who I pretended to be, I always woke up feeling empty.

I never even considered that I might have an addiction. If anything, I thought I was better with a drink or two in me—more confident, more fun, more outspoken. Sober me felt boring and quiet. If I were sober, I would probably be hungover anyway, so what was the difference? I used to wish for days when I'd feel lighter—now, in recovery, I still do, just for different reasons. I always complained that life wasn't fair, but sobriety has taught me that's just the way it is. I've spent a lot of time mad at God or whatever higher power is out there—because it's easier to blame something else than to accept my own accountability. We all look for reasons in the wreckage. Sometimes, it feels safer than facing the truth.

I had my first drink at sixteen—a swig of Pepto Bismol-pink Tequila Rose that still makes me gag thinking about it. I barely remember that night, except for puking in my best friend's bathroom and crawling down the hall while everyone laughed. You'd think I'd learned my lesson, but when the hangover wore off, I did it again. And again. I went to high school parties, drank and did whatever the crowd was doing, desperate to fit in—or maybe to stand out. I never really knew which.

Nobody calls themselves an alcoholic in their late teens or early twenties, so my partying felt normal. My twenties weren't any different—my friends drank regularly, and I just kept joining in. I was still searching for confidence, trying to fit in by being who I thought people wanted me to be. How I felt at 21 is exactly how I felt at 31: always looking for a place to belong, always afraid to just be myself.

I spent an entire decade living in amazing places with endless opportunities—and I can barely remember any of it. Maybe deep down I knew addiction was creeping in, but as long as I kept a steady job and stayed in a relationship (healthy or not), I convinced myself I was fine. I "earned" those glasses of wine after work for just making it through the day. Bingeing on weekends felt justified because I worked so hard. Even living paycheck to paycheck in a pricey Beverly Hills apartment, I had no problem dropping cash on shots and $50 lobster pizza.

Back then, I got into some truly toxic relationships—thinking my heart would never heal, not realizing alcohol was magnifying all the pain. Most of the fights weren't just about my partners; a lot of it was my own drinking and the emotions that came with it. I drank when I was sad, I drank when I was happy, and none of my partners ever really questioned it.

So, what now? I ask myself that all the time. Where do I go from here? I'm no expert, but I hope that by sharing my story— especially the messiest parts of early motherhood and addiction—I can help even one woman feel less alone, less ashamed, and maybe a little more hopeful.

When I look at my daughters—their wide eyes, their innocent trust—I realize I'm not just fighting for myself. I'm fighting for them. Because while my dad gave me a legacy of pain, I refuse to hand that down. My children will someday know my story and hopefully be proud of their mom, not ashamed of her. They'll look at me as a role model for strength through their own trials and tribulations.

I couldn't be the mom who snapped at them for spilling

my wine; I knew that wasn't really who I was. I couldn't be the mom whose absence they'd feel even while I was sitting right next to them, empty and broken inside. I couldn't be the mom they'd look back on one day and whisper, *"She loved the bottle more than she loved us."* That would never be our truth. I was and am still determined to change that narrative.

Breaking the cycle meant more than just not drinking. It meant confronting the shame, treating the trauma, defying the negative self-talk, and the belief that I wasn't enough without a glass in my hand. It meant building a new legacy—one of presence, of resilience, of showing them what it looks like to fight for yourself when it would be easier to give up. Beyond my failures and poor decisions stands a force to be reckoned with. I now embody for them the type of mother I needed and wanted for myself. The type of mother I needed growing up.

It took me a long time to stop being angry at my dad and to stop blaming him for a less-than-great childhood. To understand that he wasn't just a "bad man." He was sick. He was lost. And he never found his way out. He passed away when I was seven months pregnant with my first daughter. Sobriety has given me enough distance to hold both truths at once: he hurt me, but I also miss him. I miss the version of him I think he could have been, if only he'd gotten well. I hold space for him and his courage to face addiction, attending treatment time after time.

That grief fuels me. Because if I don't change, if I don't fight, then my daughters could be writing this same story thirty years from now about me. And I refuse to let that be their legacy.

I want my daughters to grow up with a different story. One where they remember a mom who showed up, even on the hard days. A mom who cried when she needed to but kept going anyway. A mom who taught them that feelings aren't something to drown, they're something to embrace. The good ones and the not-so-good ones.

I want them to see that mistakes don't define you—what you do next does. The importance of action vs. reaction.

And maybe someday, when they're grown and face their own storms, they'll remember that their mom didn't just survive. She rebuilt.

Addiction took so much from me. But it won't take them because this is where the curse ends. With me.

Sitting comfortably in my two years of sobriety, I know this: shame is a liar. It told me I was a bad mom, a broken wife, a failed human. That I was undeserving and incapable of loving unconditionally and accepting it back. Sobriety told me the truth: I am a work in progress, and that's okay – I will never be done working. I still stumble. I've relapsed. I've wanted to quit. But every day, I choose to stay. For my kids. For myself. For the woman I'm still becoming. For the woman I know deep down I am meant to be. The lessons I've learned just about myself continue to impress me. I didn't know then what I know now.

The shame I carried was thick, heavy, woven into my skin. I gave it life and let it continue to live with me. It told me I didn't deserve forgiveness, that every mistake was a permanent stain. But recovery has taught me something radical: mistakes are not proof of failure—they're evidence of trying. And trying is the bravest thing we do. Holding ourselves accountable? Holy shit, not everyone can do that, so bravo if you're out there and acknowledging your downfalls.

There are still hard mornings when I wake up and feel the ache in my chest, the whispers of old habits calling me back. But now, instead of reaching for a drink, I reach for my children, for my breath, for the quiet knowing that I am not the woman I used to be. And for now, that's enough. I step outside and let my bare feet touch the grass. I feel the sun warm my face and the wind whisper comfort through me. I call on God, the Universe, and whatever/whoever is out there listening to keep fueling my fire for me. And then I let it go and believe that they will. I don't obsess about it and worry about it from that moment on.

If my story reaches even one mother standing at the edge of her own breaking point, whispering in the dark, "I can't do this," then telling my story was worth it. You are not alone, and I genuinely hope you feel that and believe it. You are not broken. You are not beyond saving. You do not need to be fixed, and you are not your addiction. You are loved, even in your messiest, most unlovable moments. And you are worth every ounce of the fight it takes to come back home to yourself. Hold onto that feeling and don't let it go with everything you've got.

You are not your father or your mother. You will be the one to break the chains and lay the new foundation for your children.

One of my best friends of over 20 years passed just three months ago. What do she and my dad have in common? They were both alcoholics, and their addiction is what ultimately took them too soon. My friend was only 41 years old when she lay in a hospital bed, blood trickling down the corner of her mouth, alone, dying. And while she had been getting her stomach drained for years and knew her organs had failed her, she couldn't manage to put the bottle down. Alcohol took away her opportunities and possibilities for the beautiful life she could've lived. It took away our friendship.

In reality, she chose to give those things up. She chose alcohol over her own life. She couldn't find her way out. She kept making that choice until her addiction grew to where it was no longer a choice, and she was no longer willing.

That's a tricky thing about this disease: it's hard to be mad at someone who's died because of their drinking, but it feels impossible not to. When you have to grieve through sobriety, you feel the heaviness of survival. Almost like a guilt that sits on your shoulders. Why was I able to choose a different path in life, to pick sobriety, and she wasn't? Why couldn't she just quit? How far down was her rock bottom, or did she even have one?

Death – her rock bottom was death, and it ultimately would've been mine had I not gotten out from under it. We're not all that lucky. Even in stage four cirrhosis, with her body turning against her and shutting down, she still drank. I'm bitter that we weren't able to maintain our friendship because I couldn't allow her into my life, given the lifestyle choices she was making. I didn't want to watch her die. I didn't want to witness her killing herself. I didn't want my children to meet her or know her in case someday they might ask about what happened to her.

Man…Death sucks. Addiction sucks. Truth is, though, we're not all gonna make it to the other side of this. People we love and desperately want in our lives will succumb to this horrible disease, and there's not a damn thing we can do about it. We do, however, hold the power (and what a power that is) to change the trajectory of our own lives. To pick a different path and prove to ourselves that we are strong and capable of doing the hard work. We're the survivors, and there should be no guilt in that. Let that shit go.

Now that the dust from her death has settled for my heart and my mind, I see that my feelings of anger towards her are unwarranted. Yes, she basically killed herself, but she wasn't herself. It wasn't HER that did it. It was the disease and the version of her that it created within it. We all know the unfortunate power alcohol has over our actions and decisions, how often the things we do and say under the influence don't make any sense. How it alters our brain chemistry and the way we move through our days. I can't blame her for that; I can't be mad. I knew I was making horrible and potentially fatal decisions daily, and yet I kept making them. Would I want that judgment displaced towards me? Hell no. I wasn't in my right mind.

When you tell yourself you're moderating or cutting back, do you believe you could do it? You might have gotten into an accident or got a DUI and thought, " Phew, it could've been worse, but I'm still ok." No, the fuck you're not. There's no grey in the spectrum of alcoholism; it is black and white – don't let anyone tell you any different. You can't be an alcoholic and "cut back." You simply can't drink, not a drop, not a whisper, or a wink of alcohol can enter your bloodstream, or it's over, sister. You can't handle it, and you've gotta be ok with that. Knowing that you can't touch the stuff ever again. Admitting that you wave the white flag in its face, saying ok, you win that fight, but I'm winning this war.

There will come a time in your journey where drinking and everything surrounding it won't consume your thoughts. You won't wake up with it on your mind or fall asleep dreaming of what could've been had you been able to just have one. We're a different breed out here, and not everyone can be in this pack. Think of yourself like a wolf with a silent group of fighters behind you in your corner, but you and you alone are the sole opponent in the fight against the drink when you come face to face.

Sad shit is going to happen once you get sober, and when it does, at least the first time, you're going to feel like a fucking mess. I had no idea what to do with my emotions, shit, I don't even really know if I understood what I was feeling since it was the first time in my adult life that I was feeling them sober. It's a very strange and surreal feeling to be so present and aware. But man, what a beautiful thing to come out of a sad situation. Your brain feels less strained, and you're so much more open and honest with yourself, you probably don't even realize it as it's happening.

If you're not ready, you can't recover. Pause and read that again. **If you're not ready, you can't recover.** But if you're anything like me, you're more ready than you think. You've probably read these words and agreed with some of what I said or seen yourself within my story. That, my friend, means you're ready. Don't fight that feeling. Don't push it down and ignore it. Embrace it. Allow yourself to feel all the feelings that come, and then jump in. It isn't an ending. It's the art of staying—through grief, through joy, through everything that once sent you running. This is where *Mother Anonymous* becomes *Mother Awoken.*

Let's Reflect

1. What patterns or beliefs from your family line are you consciously breaking?

2. What do you want your children to feel when they think of you—not what you did, but who you were?

3. How has motherhood changed now that you're no longer performing survival?

4. What lessons do you hope your children learn from your healing—not your perfection?

5. When you imagine your family line generations from now, what energy do you hope still carries your name?

Let's Affirm It

You are not repeating the story—you are rewriting it.

Statistically Speaking

Genetic factors account for approximately 40%–60% of a person's risk for developing Alcohol Use Disorder (AUD). (Source: National Institute on Alcohol Abuse and Alcoholism)

Part Ten: Let's Get Real

"I had to relearn how to live and to love myself once I got sober. I have more respect and compassion for myself now than I ever have."

–Katie S., mother of one, sober two years

Sobriety didn't make me a perfect mom. It made me a *real* one. Sometimes, real looks like me crying for no known reason and walking away for a minute. It looks like I'm counting down the minutes until bedtime, so I can have some reprieve.

It also looks like dancing in the living room to Wheels on the Bus with my daughters until we're breathless with giggles. It looks like remembering what I said the night before. It looks like being proud of the woman my girls are watching me become.

I still have hard days—days when everything feels like too much, and I fantasize about running away to a hotel room with blackout curtains and no one else around. But I know those moments will pass. I sit with them, survive them, and do it all without a drink.

Because here's the truth: the hard stuff didn't disappear when I quit drinking. But neither did I. I actually started showing up.

Sobriety didn't hand me a happily-ever-after. It handed me work. It gave me more challenges to overcome and realizations to work through. It didn't make life easier; it made it more manageable. More tolerable.

The dishes still pile up. There are still snacks and kinetic sand all over my floor. There are loads of laundry being ignored. My kids still scream about the wrong color cup or the fact that their sister looked at them funny. My marriage didn't magically heal. Bills didn't stop coming. Life didn't suddenly become soft-focus and Instagram-worthy.

But here's the thing: I'm here for it now. Present. Awake. Unnumbed. And that, more than anything, is what recovery has given me. That is what will continue to get me through this. That is what makes it all worth it.

I find myself thinking back to that night in the nursery,

barefoot at 3 a.m., when everything seemed to be falling apart. Those quiet hours, surrounded by the scent of diaper cream and Dreft, and lit by the faint glow of the Hatch, were the beginning of my journey. Now, with sober eyes, I can return to that moment with a sense of peace and acceptance. What once felt like a prison of self-doubt and fear is now a place where I discovered my strength. It's in that barefoot vulnerability that I began to rewrite my story and find hope.

People like to paint sobriety as this shiny finish line: you quit drinking, and then everything falls into place. That you'll lose weight and land this amazing new job. That you'll wake up every morning filled with nothing but joy and perfect relationships. But that's bullshit. Sobriety isn't the finish line. It's the starting line. The real work begins after you put down the glass. And then, maybe, those aforementioned things can start to work their way into your life. Only then will you be able to be open enough to let it start happening and actually recognize it when it works.

And let me tell you—it's messy. My God, it's messy. It's crying in your car after preschool drop-off. It's learning how to have a fight with your partner without storming off to pour a drink. It's being fully present for your kids when you'd rather escape into a buzz. It's relearning how to live, one raw, awkward day at a time. And as the days go by, it'll all become more manageable. Life around you won't seem so intimidating and large.

These days, sobriety shows up in the small things. It's in the smiles and hugs my children run to give me. Dance parties are kind of our thing now, and rather than being irritated at my kids for climbing all over me, I encourage it. It looks like remembering what I said the night before and not having to apologize to anyone. It looks like writing my story instead of hiding behind it. It looks like being proud of the woman my girls are watching me become.

Sobriety also looks like cravings sometimes. Like wishing I could numb out. Like sitting on the floor, whispering, *"You're okay, you're okay, you're okay"* to myself until the wave passes.

It's not glamorous. But it's real.

Addiction stole years from me. It hollowed out my ambition, warped my self-worth, and nearly cost me my family. But sobriety has given me something else: clarity. And in that clarity, I see I'm not alone.

We are living in a culture that tells moms the only way to survive is to drink and to lean on everyone around you. That society supports you. That wine is the reward for exhaustion. Alcohol is the salve for stress. And yet, the truth is, it's a trap—one designed to keep us quiet, compliant, numb, and prisoner.

My story isn't unique. That's the saddest and most hopeful part. Saddest, because so many women are drowning silently, just like I did. Hopeful, because if I can crawl my way out, so can you.

Sobriety didn't fix everything. But it gave me the chance to fix myself. It gave me the chance to rewrite the story my daughters will inherit. It gave me the chance to be here and to own my life.

And that's the choice I keep making. Every second of every day.

If you are standing in your kitchen right now, staring at a half-empty glass and whispering, *"I can't do this,"* know this: you can. Not because it's easy. Not because it's pretty. But because you are stronger than you think.

You don't need a perfect plan. You don't need to believe

in yourself yet. You just need to believe in the possibility of something better.

Sobriety is not about becoming perfect. It's about becoming real. And real is enough.

So if my story does anything, I hope it's this: that it makes you feel a little less alone. That makes you whisper to yourself, *"If she can, maybe I can too."*

Because that's how we break the cycle. That's how we build something better. That's how we carry each other home.

I was going to do something big, live big. I was going to live loudly, bravely, brilliantly. And then, little by little, I handed that girl over to a glass, a bottle, a night out, a morning after. The ambition faded into the background, replaced by plans that revolved around the next drink, the next party, the next escape.

The most devastating part isn't even the lost opportunities— it's the erosion of self-trust. The way you start breaking promises to yourself so casually, you almost don't notice. The way you become two people: the one everyone sees and the one you carry inside, bruised and stumbling and gasping for air. I lied to myself more skillfully than I lied to anyone else, convincing myself that I was fine, I was fun, I was functioning.

The truth is, I wasn't fine. I was numbing. I was grieving a version of myself I didn't know how to become. And the tragedy is, the people around me—some of them saw, some of them didn't, but none of them could pull me out. That was work only I could do.

I look back now and wonder: what could have been different? Could one conversation, one intervention, one honest moment have changed the course? Or was this always the road I had to walk to get here, to this reckoning, to this raw, trembling place where I finally call the thing by its name?

I don't have the answer. But I know this: what addiction took from me was real, but what I build in its place will be real, too. And maybe—just maybe—that's where the redemption begins.

I started to ask myself the hard questions that you, too, should be asking yourself if you're still struggling:

Why do you need this?

What are you trying to avoid feeling?

Who are you without alcohol?

I didn't love the answers, and you might not either, but keep asking.

If you're holding this book, you've walked with me through

some of the darkest, rawest, and most honest moments of my life. You've seen what it means to break, to rebuild, and to choose hope again and again. I hope, more than anything, that you finish these pages with the gentle reminder that you are not alone. Whatever you're facing—addiction, heartbreak, grief, or simply the everyday overwhelm—you are worthy of grace, healing, and a new beginning.

My story is proof that cycles can be broken and that healing is always possible, no matter how many times you have to start over. If my struggles and victories have resonated with you, I ask you to choose yourself today: reach out for support, share your story, or simply take one small step toward the life you want. There is power in vulnerability, and a whole community is waiting to welcome you. You deserve a life that feels like your own.

Let's Reflect

1. What grief has surfaced now that you can finally feel everything clearly?

2. Which parts of your old life are you still mourning, even as you build a new one?

3. How does it feel to experience joy without needing to escape it—or fear it won't last?

4. What does "moving forward" mean to you now—not as an escape, but as a continuation?

5. Who are you becoming when you no longer need to be anyone's version of "okay"?

Let's Affirm It

Healing doesn't mean it never hurts again.

Statistically Speaking

Studies show that emotional regulation and resilience significantly increase within two years of sustained sobriety, even as individuals report continued grief over "lost time" or relationships. (Source: American Journal of Psychology & Recovery, 2024)

Author's Note

Writing this book was both the hardest and most healing journey I've ever taken. Putting my truth on the page meant reliving pain but also rediscovering hope—one sentence at a time. If you found comfort, courage, or even a moment of recognition in these chapters, know that connection is what I value most. I would love to hear your story, your questions, or simply your thoughts about how these words met you where you are.

If you wish to connect, share your journey, or simply say hello, please reach out. Healing happens in community, and I am honored to be a small part of yours.

With gratitude,

Amanda Tilper

amandatilper@gmail.com

Acknowledgements

To the people who stood close enough to see the mess and close enough to witness the rebuilding, this book is as much yours as it is mine.

Piper and Tilly — My girls. My heartbeat. My why. You saved me without even meaning to. You survived me while I figured out how to become someone worth surviving. You gave me the courage to stop disappearing and the reason to rise every single time I fell. Every page of this book is braided with you. I wrote my way back to myself so I could be the mother you deserve.

Peter — Our story isn't simple, and neither is this gratitude. Thank you for being part of the chaos, the conflict, and the rebuilding in ways that shaped me into someone stronger, clearer, and more honest. We weathered a storm—sometimes together, sometimes on opposite shores—but we're both still standing.

Mom — For every late-night phone call, every "just checking in," and every moment you carried what I couldn't. You loved me even when I was unlovable, and somehow made it look simple. Thank you for the quiet ways you kept me tethered when I was sure I'd drift away.

Nicole — You were steady when everything else was spinning. You told the truth without making me feel like I was breaking. You reminded me of my strength on the days I couldn't find it. Thank you for seeing the whole picture and still choosing to stay in it with me these past *"19 years."*

To my closest friends — the ones who didn't just say "let me know if you need anything," but actually meant it. You showed up in big ways, small ways, and sometimes in ways I didn't appreciate until much later. Thank you for sticking around through the parts of me that weren't pretty, convenient, or easy to love. You know exactly who you are.

And to the version of me who didn't give up — thank you for holding on long enough to write this.

We do recover.